The Healthy Pastor
Easing the Pressures of Ministry

Dennis Bickers

BEACON HILL PRESS
OF KANSAS CITY

Printed in the
United States of America

Cover Design: Darlene Filley
Interior Design: Sharon Page

Library of Congress Cataloging-in-Publication Data

Bickers, Dennis W., 1948-
    The healthy pastor : easing the pressures of ministry / Dennis Bickers.
        p. cm.
    Includes bibliographical references (p.   ).
    ISBN 978-0-8341-2553-7 (pbk.)
    1. Clergy—Job stress. I. Title.
    BV4398.B53 2010
    248.8'92—dc22

                                                                2010028986

10 9 8 7 6 5 4 3 2 1

Dedication

This book was written during a very stressful time in my life. Some of the stresses I was feeling were ministry related and are discussed in this book. Many of the stresses were related to other challenges I was facing. That year turned out to be the most difficult year of my life. When my wife learned I was writing this book during that time, she asked, "How could you write that book while going through all the things you've been going through?" Some days as I sat down in front of my computer to write, I asked myself the same question. The answer can be summed up in two words: "God" and "Faye" (my wife).

During the most difficult days there were times when I wondered if God had abandoned me, but even when I felt that way, I knew the answer was that he had not. He was the same faithful God he had always been, and I knew in my heart that he would lead me through this time in my life. All that I am or ever will be is because of his grace.

No one on this side of heaven knows all I went through that year except for my wife. She walked with me through every challenge I faced. She sat up with me many nights when I could not sleep and talked me through my emotions until I could finally lay down. She prayed for me, and she continually reminded me that together we would get through the challenges that were before us. Without God's grace and Faye's unconditional love this book would not exist, and I would not be the person I am today.

Faye, this book is dedicated to you. I will always love you.

Contents

Acknowledgments

Once again I find myself indebted to Beacon Hill Press of Kansas City for their willingness to produce another of my books. This is my fourth book with Beacon Hill, and as always they have been great to work with. I also need to thank Richard Buckner, who has edited all four of these books. He knows my stuff better than I do! He challenges me to think and write more clearly and lets me know when I've written something that may not say what I want to say. The result of his work is a book that is much better than the original manuscript I sent him.

In my last book I mentioned how much I appreciate our executive minister, Larry Mason, for allowing me the freedom to write and lead conferences around the country. He allows me to take time away from my normal responsibilities because he has a kingdom perspective of ministry. Some judicatory leaders can only see the churches for which they are responsible, but Larry is committed to the kingdom and gives our staff much leeway to do work that benefits all churches. He recently announced his retirement effective at the end of this year, and I will miss him. I would be remiss if I didn't thank him one last time for allowing me the opportunity to write and speak.

Let me also say a word of thanks to the bivocational and small church leaders who receive my monthly newsletter, read my blog, and attend the workshops I lead. I appreciate their commitment to the task God has given them. In a world that glorifies the big and flashy it's not easy to serve in the smaller places God sometimes gives us. You inspire me with your dedication to your calling.

Introduction

In a recent one-week period three pastors asked me to help them find new places to serve. One discovered that a small faction in the church planned to call for a vote of confidence at an upcoming business meeting. The other two had received word that their churches' finance committees were proposing substantial cuts to their salary and benefit packages. Two of these pastors had young children still at home. The third had faithfully served his church for several years.

During this same time, I sat with a pastor whose slumped shoulders had already told me what he was about to say. He was tired. He was frustrated. He had served his church for over two decades, but he was wishing retirement was much closer than it was. He did not feel led to leave his church, but he was just so tired.

Just the day before that meeting, I met with another pastor who was closer to retirement age. He had never planned to take early retirement, but the pressures of ministry were becoming too difficult. Former supporters in his church were turning against him. Rumors were flying around the congregation and community. Even though the stories were not true, they still hurt. By the end of our meeting he had decided to announce to his leadership board that he would retire in a few months when he turned sixty-two.

Ministry has always been challenging, but the pressures seem to be increasing in our society with its high expectations and pursuit of immediate gratification. These pressures are taking a high toll on the health and well-being of many pastors, their families, and the churches they serve. Clergy now have the second-highest divorce rate among all professionals.[1] Nearly half of the ministers in a poll conducted by Focus on the Family reported they had experienced depression or burnout so severe that they had to take a leave of absence from the ministry.[2] This burnout is one reason why approximately half of seminary graduates leave the ministry within five years after graduation.[3] With so many clergy leaving the ministry, many churches, especially smaller ones, are finding it difficult to find quality pastoral leadership.

Many of the pressures clergy face are due to the unrealistic expectations placed on them. George Barna's research found that church members expect their pastor to be able to juggle an average of sixteen different tasks.[4] No minister can meet such unrealistic expectations, but many of them try. In fact, some ministers have expectations of themselves that are just as unrealistic. They believe they are to be all things to all people and be able to meet every expectation that exists in the congregations they serve.

Other pressures of ministry are not caused by expectations but are often challenges faced by most ministers because of their work. Issues such as being alone, managing time, and having to address the rapid changes in our society put tremendous pressure on many clergypersons.

The stresses from the many different pressures our clergy now face are driving many away from God's call on their lives. The wounded ones who remain often do so out of a sense of duty, having lost the joy of their call years earlier. Some of their spouses have learned to hate the church, and their children are not only bitter toward the church but also toward their minister parents who allowed the church to treat their families as it did.

What must happen? First, we must name the pressures clergy experience and expose them for what they are. This book will explore a number of pressures that nearly every minister will face sometime in his or her ministry. Second, we need to teach both churches and clergy how to address each of these pressures in healthier ways. Each chapter of this book will attempt to do that. After identifying a pressure that ministers face, we will look at how it can be eliminated or, at least, better managed. Third, we must educate some churches that they need to carefully examine and determine if their expectations for clergy leadership are unrealistic and unnecessarily stressful on ministers and their families.

Let me be very blunt at this point. Some churches do not deserve a pastor. I call such churches widow-makers. They are so unhealthy and have such unrealistic expectations for their ministers that they are not only driving ministers out of the ministry but also causing some to develop serious physical, emotional, and even spiritual problems. Trying to meet the expectations of such churches causes ministers to sacrifice their health, their families, and their future ministry opportunities.

If you are a pastor in such a church, you need to begin praying about whether or not you need to stay in such an environment. I once worked nightshift in a factory for a supervisor who feared the pressures the company put on him were causing him physical problems. I told him he needed to make some changes because if he fell over with a heart attack, someone would put him in a chair and call the in-plant ambulance to take him to the hospital, but the assembly line would never shut down. If he died, he would be replaced within a week, but his family would miss him forever. The next night he collapsed. Sure enough, someone put him in a chair and called the ambulance. The assembly line never stopped. Fortunately, he had not had a heart attack. His collapse was stress related, and the doctor told him he needed to reduce his stress or he would suffer something far worse the next time. Since the stress of his position was not going to improve, he had to find a new job to protect himself and his family. Ministers should not feel that being deeply spiritual means sacrificing their health and families to serve a congregation that does not seem to care about either.

If you are a lay leader reading this book, I encourage you to honestly evaluate the pressures your church places on your ministers. What are your church's expectations? Are they realistic? One way to evaluate this is by looking at the average tenure of your ministers and the reasons they left your church. If you find they are leaving in three to five years, with issues always surrounding their leaving, then your church probably has unrealistic expectations. This must change if your church ever hopes to be healthy and have a vital ministry in your community.

Not all unrealistic expectations are found in the church. Some persons enter the ministry with unrealistic expectations of the ministry and the churches they serve. In such cases pressures do not come from the churches but from the ministers. Just as some churches are harmful to the clergy who serve them, some ministers leave a trail of destruction and disappointment behind in every church they serve. Such ministers need to repent of the damage they have done in church after church and seek to learn healthier ways of relating to churches.

Finally, we in judicatory ministry have a responsibility to our churches and ministers to help them address the pressures in their relationships. We cannot continue to sacrifice good ministers on the altars of churches that care nothing about them or the pressures they and their families face. Moreover, we cannot allow unhealthy ministers to bring harm to every church they serve. We have to address the pressures that are causing too many of our ministers to abandon the call of God on their lives so that both they and the churches they serve can experience more fruitful ministries.

One of the working titles I considered for this book was *Avoiding the Stresses of Ministry*, until I realized that no one can ever avoid the stresses of ministry. As in any occupation, there are stresses that go with the responsibility, and they will always be there. The good news is that these stresses can be alleviated. With some careful planning, good communication, and a little cooperation the stresses experienced by many in the ministry can be reduced, some can be eliminated, and the minister can recapture the joy and excitement that was first felt when he or she entered the ministry.

Pressures of Family

During a gathering of pastors and their spouses H. B. London Jr. asked, "What is the greatest frustration you face in church ministry?" One minister's wife wrote,

> Loneliness, lack of spiritual kinship with other women, "single" parenting, powerful women in the church bossing my husband around, lack of finances, and identity crisis. I am a non-person, not my husband's partner in ministry, not a full-fledged member. I'd like to get a lot of stuff going in the church, but I have to defer.[1]

Other complaints spouses of clergy often voice is the pressure of living in a fishbowl, especially if they reside in the church parsonage; interruptions at mealtimes; unrealistic expectations some congregation members have for the minister's spouse; the long hours too many ministers work each week; and the expectation that spouses are to set aside their feelings and needs for the good of the church. Some spouses feel the church is in competition with them for the attentions of their husbands or wives in ministry, which makes their frustration even worse. They could fight for their husbands or wives against other threats to marriage, but how can they fight against the church without appearing to be fighting God?

Lynne Hybels understands the feeling. In the days before her husband, Bill, started Willow Creek Community Church, he was the leader of a youth ministry called Son City. It was a demanding ministry that kept him away from his new bride much of the time. Recalling one evening she writes,

> Another lonely meal. Another empty evening. An hour earlier I had begged Bill to stay home. He had looked at me with disbelief. "Kids are dying and going to hell, and you want me to stay home and hold

your hand?" I am too young and too insecure to know how to respond. . . . Six months into marriage, I am convinced I have made a
horrible mistake. I love the man I married. I love Son City. But I hate
our marriage. I hate the pain of disappointment. I hate mourning
the death of so many dreams. And I hate the loneliness.[2]

Children Feel the Pain Too

Several years ago a movie on TV told the story of a woman who led
her city in an effort to help young people with drug problems. As she
went about her work in the community, she failed to notice her own
daughter reaching out to her. One evening on her way home, she saw
messages painted on the sidewalks claiming that her daughter was using drugs. She was furious and knew someone was out to destroy her
reputation and the work she was doing. Her anger built as she continued home, but when she walked in the house she noticed a paintbrush
and a can of paint the same color as the sidewalk messages. It was the
only way her daughter could get her mother's attention. She had to
become one of the people her mother wanted to rescue.

Could it be that some children of ministers develop the problems
they do in order to get noticed by their clergy parents? Could others
be rebelling against the teachings of the church in order to strike back
at the organization they believe is responsible for taking their father or
mother away from the important events of their lives? I believe either
scenario is possible. More than one minister's child has carried bitter-
ness and anger against God and the church into adult life for the harm
done to his or her family by the demands of ministry.

The Minister's Family Is Unique

We recognize that every family has problems from time to time.
Husbands and wives disagree about many things regardless of profession. Children and their parents will always have issues they have to
work through. But there are problems found in ministers' families that
are not found in many other homes.

A minister's family relates more to his or her profession than normally occurs with any other professions.[3] In a doctor's home, few family members go to the hospital or office to watch the doctor practice
medicine. Seldom will the family members of a CPA go to the office
to watch him or her prepare tax statements. However, the minister's
family can be found in church almost every Sunday watching the min-

ister perform his or her responsibilities. Family members watch how other people respond to the leadership of the minister, and they may be uncertain how to relate to this person who seems larger than life. Tim Stafford wrote about what it was like growing up as the child of a minister: "If your father is the public's person, then it is difficult to have him for your own. He can become more of a symbol, a totem, than a person. You are never quite sure what is real and what is not. He becomes an idealized version of a father. Or, he becomes a hypocrite in your eyes, unable to make his private and public lives match."[4]

The family sees a side of the minister that most of the congregation never sees. They see the hurt and disappointment that comes when people do not follow through. They witness the behind-the-scenes anger when difficult people continue to challenge and block the minister's every effort to make positive changes in the church. They hear the comments at the dinner table about problems and people at the church. The spouse may be able to distinguish the public pastor from the private person, but that does not mean the children are able to do so.

Family as Unpaid Staff

The congregation members may have expectations for the minister's family that they do not have for other families in the church. Some churches expect the pastor's family to serve as unpaid staff. The spouse may be expected to prepare church bulletins, handle certain secretarial duties, or answer incoming calls, especially when the parsonage phone number is the same as that of the church. One of the old jokes of pastor search committees used to be that a candidate had to have a spouse who played the piano. But this was no joke to one committee, who admitted to me that they actually thought it be would be very helpful to find a pastor whose wife could play the piano for their worship service.

Many ministers' spouses work outside the home, just as is the case for many families in the congregation who have both the husband and wife working outside the home. Often this is a necessity for ministers because of their low income. We will address that in greater detail in the next chapter. However, in many cases, the spouse may be working in a career of his or her choosing. He or she may feel called to this work just as the minister feels called to the ministry. He or she may have invested years in education preparing to work in a certain field. Churches who believe that the spouse of their pastor should not work outside the home are simply not being realistic about the changes that have occurred in recent times.

To be sure, both men and women are called to ministry positions (that is why inclusive language is used throughout this book), but for many years churches called only male pastors. Congregations in turn saw the primary role of pastors' wives to be raising children, supporting their husbands, and doing whatever the church needed them to do. Many churches frowned on the idea of the wife working outside the home, because that would take her away from those primary responsibilities. It also told the world one of two things—that the church did not pay enough to support the pastor and his family or that the family was greedy and simply wanted more money. Either option would be an embarrassment to the church. While these were expectations of many churches in the past, and are no longer realistic today, many people in our churches still adhere to them.

Such expectations, while depriving the minister's family of much-needed income in some cases, can also rob a spouse of his or her identity as a person created in the image of God and gifted and equipped by him for service. That service may take place outside the church and in the marketplace as the spouse works in the professional, clerical, retail, or industrial world. Any attempt to deprive the minister's spouse of his or her identity as a person of worth and ability will add great stress to the minister's family.

Family members of the minister must be allowed to find their own level of involvement in the life of the church without pressure from the church. Some spouses will be comfortable taking leadership positions in the church, while others will prefer working more in the background because of their temperaments and personalities. Some may be involved in many different activities, while others may be limited by the demands of family and/or careers. The level of involvement must be determined by the minister and his or her family, not the congregation.

Stresses Related to Housing

If the church has a parsonage, there can be stresses related to that. Some church members believe they have the right to come into the parsonage any time they want, since "this house belongs to the church." Other churches expect to have Sunday school classes meet in the parsonage or that it will be available for committee meetings. There can be issues with repairs and upkeep. Some churches modernize their parsonages based upon the wishes of their current pastor and family, and some refuse to update or improve anything. In one extreme case a minister and his wife had to sleep in their camper because the church would not resolve a serious mold problem in the parsonage. In some churches, getting approval to change the color schemes in the parsonage can be a problem, even if the pastor and family agree to do the painting.

Some churches require their ministers to live in the parsonage to exercise control over them. If congregation members can tell the pastor where to live, they may be able to dictate other areas of his or her life as well. The minister may be less likely to create problems in the church knowing that if he or she is forced to leave, his or her family may have no place to live. One pastor lived in a parsonage next door to the church, and he was constantly being watched by congregation members who lived across the street. Because the church paid the utility bills, he was even once asked why he left his lights on so late at night. A controlling church with a parsonage can create enormous stress in the life of its minister and his or her family.

Many churches have sold their parsonages, which can also create stresses for the minister's family. Young ministers just starting out may not have the down payment needed for a mortgage. Their salaries may not be enough to make monthly payments on a house suitable to their needs, especially if the housing costs are high in that part of the country. They may have to settle for a smaller home than they need and find that a growing family quickly requires additional space. If they cannot afford to purchase a larger home, they will begin to experience a number of stresses from feeling trapped by their circumstances, especially if most of the congregation members seem able to live comfortably in their homes.

Stresses Related to Time

An entire chapter will be devoted to time management for ministers, but one of the common stresses for the minister's family is the time he or she is away from home and family activities. Meals are often interrupted by telephone calls. Meetings may be scheduled at the church every night of the week. There are hospital and home visits to make, sermons to prepare, special programs to develop and oversee, and a to-do list that never seems to get done. Many ministers' families feel they get whatever time is left over, and there never seems to be any left over.

Vacations are cut short due to church members dying and the minister returning to conduct the funeral. Ball games, dance recitals, and school functions are missed because a member of the congregation has gone to the emergency room and the family has requested the minister to come right away. Weekend getaways are out of the question, although others in the church never seem to have a problem finding the time for such excursions.

Fishbowl Living

Many ministers' families complain of feeling like they live in a fishbowl. They feel that everyone in the church is watching them and evaluating their actions and attitudes. They may feel as though everyone in the church has an opinion about how they dress, how they wear their hair, what music they listen to, who their friends are, how they conduct themselves in public and in the church, and how they spend their spare time. Such constant attention is grossly unfair. No one else in the church gets scrutinized like the minister's family. It also creates a lot of tension and causes resentment against the church. Some ministers' families have reported that they feel as if they can never measure up to the expectations of the congregation, and they resent that they even need to.

Reducing the Stresses Felt by the Family

Regardless of a person's profession, stresses in the home impact effectiveness and create numerous problems in other areas of life. We have an obligation to protect our family members from unrealistic expectations no matter where those expectations come from. Being called to the ministry does not negate that obligation. One of the beliefs I had throughout my ministry is that if I became the pastor of the largest church in the world but lost my family, I would have failed as a minister. How can the stresses felt by the family of a minister be reduced and even eliminated? There are several things that can help achieve this.

Communication

Some of the questions I always asked pastor search committees had to do with the involvement of previous pastors' families in the life of the church and what expectations the church had about such involvement. A pastor must know this before accepting the call to a church so there are no surprises after he or she gets there. I knew the activities my wife would be comfortable doing in a church and those she would not be comfortable doing. If a church had expectations that would put undue stress on her or on us, we accepted that as a sign that this was not the right church for us. My questions allowed us to determine that before accepting a call to the church.

I regularly communicated to the congregation and to church leaders about the priority I gave to my family. I reminded them that their church had many pastors before me and would likely have many after me, but I was the only husband my wife would ever have, and I was the only father our children would ever know. I was responsible before God to minister to their needs just as I was to minister to the church. Our church never resented my commitment to our family, and they even seemed to appreciate that commitment.

A Spouse Should Have His or Her Own Identity

A minister's ministry should not determine the identity of his or her spouse. The minister's spouse is a person created in the image of God with unique talents and abilities. He or she has goals and dreams that have also been given by God. Just as the minister has been called into the ministry, so has the minister's spouse a unique calling to fulfill. A minister has a right to expect a spouse to be supportive in the work God has given him or her to do, but a spouse also has a right to expect support from the minister. And that support needs to be publicly stated to the church.

Admittedly, this can sometimes be difficult for a church to accept, depending on the calling a spouse may have. Congregation members of one church struggled with their pastor's wife being called to pastor in another church of a different denomination. They had even more problems with the pastor's children preferring their mother's church over them, and their pastor permitted his children to attend the church they preferred. Sufficient conflict arose so that the pastor felt it necessary to resign and begin seeking another place to serve. To do anything less would have robbed his wife of her own sense of identity and self-worth and would have defrauded her of the opportunity to serve God according to the call he has on her life.

Children Should Be Allowed to Be Children

I frequently told our children that they never had to do anything just because they were the pastor's children. I did expect them to make good choices because they were the right choices to make, but they never had to feel that they were pressured into doing anything because they were children of a minister. A couple of times during my pastorate I was questioned about some decision or action our children had taken, and I was always able to stand up for them and explain why they had made the choices they had made.

When our son was in high school, he had an opportunity to play on an AAU basketball team. The problem was that some of the games would be on Sunday, and he wasn't sure I would let him miss church to play. His coach assured me he would take our son to the Sunday games, since I obviously could not do so. My wife and I agreed this was a good opportunity for him, and we allowed him to play on this team. The first Sunday he missed church I explained that he was playing for an AAU basketball team, and his team had an away game that day. Some churches would have had a problem with that, but we had consistently emphasized the importance of family, and no one said a word about him being absent that morning. Later that day I came into the sanctuary for the evening service, and our son was sitting with my parents. He had returned home in time to come to church that evening, and even though he knew he didn't have to, he wanted to come to the evening service. I believe he came that evening because I had honored him as a person and allowed him to enjoy the experience of AAU basketball instead of insisting that as the pastor's son he needed to be in church.

Housing Issues

Regardless of whether the minister lives in a parsonage or rents or buys a house, that dwelling is the home of the minister and his or her family. Members of the congregation should never feel they have a right to enter that home any time they want to, nor should they think that it is a meeting place for the church. This home is a sanctuary for the minister and family to escape from the world and enjoy one another.

If the church provides a parsonage, the church should maintain it well with regular upkeep and modern appliances. Before a new pastor comes to the church, the parsonage should be cleaned, it should be freshly painted, and all appliances checked for proper operation. Carpets should be cleaned or replaced. Input from the new pastor's family should be sought before making changes to the parsonage. Congregation members of one church asked their new pastor's wife what appliances she preferred for the parsonage before replacing them. They even asked about carpet colors so that the pastor's furniture would match when the family moved in.

The church should see that repairs are made quickly. A leaking roof, electrical issues, appliance breakdowns, the lack of heating or cooling—all contribute unneeded stress to the family of the minister. The church should have money set aside in the budget and available so immediate repairs can be made.

Some churches have made the decision in recent years to sell their parsonages. Many of these parsonages have been older houses that required too much upkeep, and it was more cost effective to sell the parsonages and provide ministers with housing allowances. Some have discovered that many ministers prefer to own their homes due to the tax advantages they can enjoy and the equity they can build up in the house.

Time Issues

We will explore time issues more thoroughly in a later chapter. Here we will simply say that ministers' families deserve more than just the time left over from ministry. Ministers must set aside time to attend activities that are important to their children. They need to schedule vacation times and take them. They must set time aside for a regular date night with their spouses to keep their marriages healthy and exciting. All congregations have an idea of how ministers should spend their time, but only the ministers can determine the priorities that really matter. The ministers are the only ones who can schedule their days and weeks, and if their families are a priority to them, that will be seen in their calendars. Do plans ever get changed when emergencies occur? Of course, that is one of the stresses of ministry that will never go away. But emergencies should not be a regular part of life. If a minister always seems to be responding to an emergency, someone isn't doing a good job of planning.

If the minister's home has an answering machine, he or she doesn't have to answer the phone every time the family sits down to dinner. The machine can get the message. If it is a true emergency, the minister can pick it up or immediately call the person back. If it is just someone wanting to talk, as it usually is, the minister can return the call when it's convenient. Letting that answering machine take some of the calls will send a powerful message to the family that they are important. If a minister doesn't have an answering machine, getting one might be one of the best investments he or she can make for the family.

Escape from the Fishbowl

Ministers and their families have the right to live like normal human beings, especially since they are! As long as their clothing is tasteful and modest, it is no one's business how the minister's children dress. The same is true of the spouse. Hairstyles, the type of car a person drives, hobbies, where a person shops, the music a person enjoys, and what a person eats are all matters of personal preference and not anyone else's business.

Too many ministers' families feel suffocated by self-appointed watchdogs in the congregation who watch their every move and report their findings to anyone they think will listen. To protect the families, these watchdogs must be confronted. It is usually best if lay leaders in the church can do this confrontation, but if they are unwilling, then the ministers themselves must do it with great sensitivity and firmness. Otherwise, the families will continue to experience unneeded stress, which for ministers may cause long-term damage to their ministries and to their relationships with family members.

2
Pressures of Finances

Few things for ministers are more difficult to discuss than money. It is usually the last thing that ministers and search committees talk about when discussing a pastoral position. Many finance committees still expect the minister to leave the room when they begin to discuss the pastor's salary and benefit package for the upcoming year. It somehow seems unspiritual to some people for a minister to talk about the financial needs of his or her family. Interestingly enough, others in the church do not seem to have a problem trying to find ways to improve the financial situation of their families, but they can get very upset when ministers talk about their financial situations.

What Do Ministers Earn?

The Pulpit and Pew Research on Pastoral Leadership at Duke University released a report in 2003 based on a survey they did two years earlier that attempted to determine clergy salaries.[1] The study found there was a large difference in the median salaries between connectional churches, such as Methodists, Lutherans, Presbyterians, and Episcopalians, and the congregational churches, such as Baptists, Pentecostals, and independent churches.

	Small <100	Medium 101-350	Large 351-1,000	Mega 1,000+
Connectional	$36,000	$49,835	$66,003	
Congregational	$22,300	$41,051	$59,315	$85,518

While the salaries for the larger churches may appear to be healthy, the report also indicated that over half of the connectional pastors and almost two-thirds of the congregational pastors serve in the small church with one hundred or less in attendance. This means that over half of the clergy surveyed are at the bottom of the pay scale.

The news for women clergy is mixed in this report. The study found that women clergy made on average 90 percent of the salary of their male counterparts, $40,000 for women ministers versus $44,200 for the male ministers. When the researchers focused only on those clergy who made less than $60,000, they found that females averaged only $600 less than the males. However, they also found that women had fewer opportunities to move into the higher-paying clergy positions.

African-American ministers experienced an even greater gap between their salaries and that of the white ministers. They earned on average two-thirds of the salaries of the white ministers in this survey. They also received fewer benefits such as retirement benefits.

How Does This Compare to Other Professions?

The following information comes from a national compensation survey conducted by the United States Department of Labor to determine the salaries of various occupations in 2006.[2] This survey found that elementary and middle school teachers had a median salary of $45,805, marriage and family therapists had a median salary of $57,496, and human resource managers enjoyed a median salary of $59,155. These occupations were selected because many ministers are expected to be proficient in these tasks and numerous others in their churches and because each of them has similar educational expectations.

The Stress of Low Income

Let's try to put all this into perspective. A minister completes four years of college and an additional two to three years to earn a master's degree. According to the Association of Theological Schools nearly 18 percent of those seminary graduates leave school with student loans in excess of $40,000.[3] In addition, many of them have incurred other debt from credit cards, car loans, and other purchases they may have made. They may have married while in school and started a family. In many cases, they will begin their ministry in churches with less than one hundred people attending on average, which means, according to the charts above, that they can expect to earn between $22,300 and $36,000, depending on their denominational affiliation and geographic location. They will find it difficult to provide for their families on such salaries, much less pay back their loans. Unless the minister is bivocational or the spouse works outside the home, they will experience tremendous financial stress, driving many of them out of the ministry toward careers that will financially provide for their families.

If the minister is bivocational or the spouse works outside the home, there is likely to be stress as well because it takes precious time away from the family. I served as a bivocational minister of a church for twenty years, and I know it is a viable option, but it means making a commitment to set aside time for the family to avoid potential problems.

Other Stresses Related to Finances

Apart from the issue of low salaries paid by many of our churches, there are other financial considerations that can create major pressures in the minister's family. In the introduction I mentioned that two pastors had been told by their finance committees that new budgets would include lower salaries and/or reduced benefits. This creates great stress on a family whose standard of living is based on an expected salary level. Such action by a church also damages the self-esteem of the minister as he or she wonders why the church is not honoring his or her years of service.

In the case of the two pastors, the ministers knew that their churches had the financial ability to continue providing livable salaries, so they felt their ministries were no longer appreciated or wanted. Both ministers immediately began seeking new places to serve. One announced his resignation even before being called to another place of service because his wife was emotionally unable to return to their church. Many ministers and their families live with the fear that if the church begins having financial problems, the first place they will look to save money is with the pastor's salary and benefits.

Many pastors and their families do not have medical insurance or they have inadequate coverage. There is no question that rising health costs are having a serious impact on churches. Churches can expect to pay as much as twenty thousand dollars a year or even more to provide good medical insurance for a minister with a family. Some churches give a sum of money to their minister and tell the minister to purchase his or her own health insurance, but in many cases this sum of money is insufficient. Either the minister does not buy insurance and prays that it will not be needed or a policy is purchased with such a high deductible that it really does not benefit the minister unless there is a major medical occurrence. Families without medical insurance experience untold stress, especially if someone becomes ill.

Because many ministers live in the church parsonage, they lose out on tax advantages that home owners enjoy. They also do not benefit from the increase in value that usually happens with a house. For many Americans, their home represents their largest investment, and the sale of that home at retirement time will provide much of their retirement income. Ministers who live in parsonages do not have that to look forward to. They can also be at a disadvantage if they move to a church that does not have a parsonage. One minister had served a church with a parsonage for over twenty years. He accepted the call to another church and realized for the first time in his life he had to buy a house. He felt the stress.

Larger churches provide their ministers with a good reimbursement policy to reduce their tax burden and to relieve them of having to spend personal money on ministry-related items, but smaller churches often overlook this option. Ministers of smaller churches may spend almost as much as they earn to purchase gasoline used for ministry purposes, attend continuing education events to improve their ministry skills, purchase books and magazine subscriptions to help them stay current, and entertain church members and potential new members. This reduces the income available to meet family needs and adds more stress to the family.

Reducing the Financial Stresses

Churches must become more responsible in their support of their ministers. For many, this begins with churches making an honest appraisal of their current situation and the realities of ministry and life in the twenty-first century. Raising a family now costs much more than it did twenty or thirty years ago, and churches need to stop thinking that a pastor can support his or her family on the same salary that was sufficient for an earlier time.

When I meet with search committees to assist them in their search for a new minister, I often hear, "Well, this is all we can afford to pay our minister right now, but if the church grows, then we'll try to pay more." When I hear that I think, *These people don't want a pastor; they want a commissioned salesman.* If the pastor can convince more people to join this church and support it financially, then the church will look at increasing the salary. This way of thinking takes the entire burden off the members of the congregation, releasing them from feeling responsible for the financial well-being of the minister's family. The minister must raise the money for his or her own salary. In First Corinthians the apostle Paul made it clear that ministers should be adequately compensated for their service, and the responsibility for doing so rests upon the churches being served.

While working with a search committee with the attitude that they would try to increase the minister's salary if the church grew, I asked how long it had been since the church had any type of stewardship training. The committee chair asked, "What's stewardship?" I responded, "You just answered my question." Less than a minute into my explanation of stewardship, the chair stopped me and said, "If you're talking about me giving more money to the church, you can forget it. I'm giving all I can already." It is interesting that churches with the attitude that the pastor must grow the church in order to receive a larger salary are also the churches that most often resent any effort by the minister to teach on stewardship. They are the same ones who complain that "all the minister talks about is money."

Responsible churches need to look at their current situation and determine if they can afford to pay fair salaries to their ministers or if they need to look at alternative plans. Many churches today are realizing they need to consider becoming bivocational so their pastors can earn additional salary outside the church. This is a very responsible position to take and is a workable solution to a difficult issue. Three of my previous books have addressed the benefits associated with bivocational ministry and would be excellent resources for any church considering making this move.

Irresponsible churches will continue to expect to find persons willing to serve at such low salaries that their families suffer, they experience tremendous stress, and they find they must either leave the ministry or soon move to another church to adequately provide for their families. These churches will later complain about the quality of the persons who serve them as pastors or about not finding anyone who won't jump at the chance to go to a larger church. They will also often complain about their judicatories, who can't seem to provide them with better ministers.

Ministers also have some responsibility in this. Too many, especially when they are first starting out, are willing to accept a call to a church that they know cannot provide financially for their family needs. Much of the stress they feel is their own fault for accepting such a call. It used to be considered somewhat unspiritual for a minister to be concerned about the salary package the church offered, and some ministers still hold to that position. However, Scripture does not support that view. In 1 Tim. 5:8 we read, "But if anyone does not provide for his own, and especially for those of his household, he has denied the faith and is worse than an unbeliever."

Clergy have a spiritual obligation to ensure that the financial needs of their families are met. Clergy and the churches they serve must work together to determine a fair salary and benefit package that will reduce the stresses of unmet financial needs.

What Is a Fair Salary and Benefit Package?

The American Baptist Churches USA recommends that a church calling a fully funded minister with a seminary education should consider matching the compensation with that of an elementary school principal who has similar years of experience.[4] Some denominations set minimum salaries for their ministers based on education and years of service but then recommend that the church increase that salary based upon the salaries paid by similar size churches in the area and the salaries of other professional people with similar education.[5] The key is that the compensation paid to a minister should be comparable with that received by other similarly experienced and educated professionals in their community.

This comparison will take into account the cost of living in the community. A church in a small Midwest community will likely pay a smaller salary than a church in a major metropolitan area simply because of the difference in the cost of living. The minister's salary will also be impacted by the particular group the church is trying to reach. One relatively new church is committed to reaching the people who live in the two wealthiest areas of their city. They have purchased a home in one of those areas close to property they have purchased for the church facility. Not only is the church paying a very good salary to their pastor, but the parsonage also has a market value of eight hundred thousand dollars.

While few churches will offer parsonages that expensive, housing is an important part of a minister's compensation package. Churches without a parsonage should designate a portion of the minister's salary as housing allowance. This can be done by having the minister estimate the housing expense for the year and having the church approve this amount as housing allowance. Because a housing allowance is nontaxable, such a designation can save the minister much in taxes, but the amount must be approved in advance each year. A judicatory leader or an accountant knowledgeable about clergy taxes can assist the church in properly setting up a housing allowance.

As mentioned earlier, ministers who live in parsonages lose the opportunity to earn equity in their homes. They are unable to fund their retirement with that equity, as many Americans do, by selling their homes when they retire. Churches that provide parsonages deprive their ministers of that equity unless they find a way to return it. One church has their parsonage appraised each year, and the equity earned in that year is paid to the minister, who can put it into his savings.

Benefits

Cash salary and housing make up only one component of a minister's total compensation package. In some cases, the benefits the church offers may be almost as important as the salary, especially when it comes to health insurance. Health care coverage is becoming extremely expensive for churches to provide. Coverage for a middle-aged clergyperson with a family can exceed twenty thousand dollars a year in premiums. This is beyond the ability of many churches, and there is no expectation that these rates will decline in the immediate future. If not for the coverage ministers' spouses receive from their places of employment, many ministers and their families would be without medical insurance. This is a burden that ministers should not have to face.

Some churches have been able to purchase less expensive insurance policies with higher deductibles and co-pays, and they pay the deductibles. A church can also establish a medical flexible spending account (FSA). Using a medical FSA, an amount of tax-free money is set aside from the minister's salary to spend on medical expenses. FSAs are easy to set up, but there are some rules that must be followed, so a church would be wise to get guidance in how to establish them.

Even ministers want to retire at some time in their lives, but many find retirement difficult to fund. Few people today believe social security will provide for a livable retirement. As noted above, ministers who have lived in parsonages normally do not earn the money they would have earned from owning their homes. Salaries may have been low, making it difficult to save or invest money. To assist their ministers with retirement many denominations have created pension programs that churches and ministers can pay into. Responsible churches will want to reward their ministers with the opportunity to enjoy a comfortable retirement by paying into these pension programs.

Many churches are not aware that their ministers are considered self-employed by social security and are required to pay the full amount of social security tax. It is recommended that the church pay a social security offset of at least 50 percent of the total social security tax the minister would pay. This would be comparable to what other employers pay for their employees and what churches are required to pay for their nonordained staff.

Reimbursable Expenses

Another part of a minister's compensation package is reimbursable expenses. These typically include such things as automobile expenses, convention and continuing education expenses, books and magazines related to the ministry, and hospitality funds. Each of these must be a true reimbursable expense, or it becomes taxable income. Some churches simply say that one thousand dollars of the minister's salary is designated automobile reimbursement. The IRS will not recognize that as a reimbursement and will charge tax on that money. A receipt must be turned in for an expense actually incurred and a check written to cover that expense for it to be a true reimbursement.

Financial Pressures Can Be Reduced

Ministers and their families do not have to experience pressures related to finances if they and the churches they serve will have honest and open discussions about their financial needs. Problems are most likely to occur when this communication does not occur. As mentioned earlier, many churches still expect the minister to leave the room when the finance committee gets to the part of the budget that involves the minister's salary and benefit package. Such an expectation is immature and unnecessary and makes it appear the church has something to hide. It also prevents the minister from the opportunity to advocate for the financial needs of his or her family. This in itself can lead to greater anxiety for the minister's family because they feel there is no one speaking up for their needs.

Many judicatories need to do more to advocate for fair compensation for their clergy. This can be done through education and by challenging their churches to assume more responsibility for their minister's financial well-being.

Not only does the minister stand to benefit from honest and open communication about finances, but the church will benefit from such discussions as well. More than one congregation has lost a good minister because they refused to provide a decent salary increase or a benefit and then found the cost to call a new pastor was greater than what they could have paid their previous pastor. Not only did they sometimes have to spend more money out of pocket for their new pastor, but they also lost the momentum they were experiencing from the leadership of their previous pastor. What is the actual cost to a church that may search one to two years or more for a new pastor? How many people may leave the church during that period? What additional costs are incurred as the new pastor spends a year or two getting to know the church and creating new ministries for the church?

Churches, their ministers, and the ministers' families can all benefit from honest discussions about finances. If the church truly cannot afford to meet the financial needs of their current minister, that fact should be recognized as soon as possible and alternatives explored. Nothing can be gained if ministers and their families have continuing financial pressures that will impact the effectiveness of their ministries.

Pressures of Finding a Place to Serve

For ministers who are not placed in ministry positions by judicatory leaders, few things create as much stress as finding the church or ministry in which they will minister. Unless this is a minister's first ministry position after seminary, there is the question of whether he or she should leave a current place of ministry for another? How can a minister be certain that this is where God is leading? Who can help with the decision? What factors need to be considered? How will a move impact the minister's family?

A few years ago I was faced with this decision. After serving as a pastor of one church for twenty years, our judicatory asked me to come on staff and serve as an area minister. One advantage I had was that I did not have to address many of the issues that clergy often do when faced with a new ministry opportunity. My wife and I did not have to move from our current home and leave our family and friends. Our children were grown and on their own, so we did not have to factor them into the decision. My wife could remain at her job and not worry about trying to find a new one in a new community. Still, it was a difficult decision to make because it meant leaving a ministry and a congregation I loved.

Although seeking advice from trusted friends and family is wise, the minister is the only one who can make the actual decision, and it is perhaps the loneliest one he or she must make. In my case, those few weeks of praying and trying to decide what to do were very stressful, as were the days after I chose to accept the offer and knew I had to tell our church I was leaving.

When Should a Minister Leave a Ministry?

Every minister has been warned to never resign on Monday. There are times when a minister feels he or she just can't stay at a church one more day, but those are not the times to leave. Problems are not always a sign that it is time to dust off the résumé. Sometimes problems occur because the church is on the verge of a breakthrough into an entire new level of ministry, and the problems occur because the enemy is trying to keep that breakthrough from happening. Those problems usually have a face or two attached to them who may make ministry there extremely difficult and frustrating, but those problems probably have "relatives" in many other churches as well. A minister can't always escape them by moving. Chances are good that the church has been at the point of a breakthrough before, and these same people were the ones who prevented it from happening. Their earlier success may be because the previous minister would not stay and resist their efforts to control the church, and if the current minister leaves, they win again.

If problems are not a sign that a minister should consider moving to a new place of ministry, what are some acceptable indicators for such a move? If a minister and the congregation have competing visions for the church, that would be an indicator that it is time to leave. Many, perhaps most, churches are stuck in a maintenance mentality. They are more committed to survival than to ministry and will do nothing to jeopardize their survival. Here we are not talking about a handful of people resisting change; we are talking about the entire church resisting any effort to follow the minister's leading into new ways of ministering.

I first shared this story in *Intentional Ministry in a Not-So-Mega Church,* but it is such a common problem and so pertinent to this discussion that it bears repeating. A couple of years ago I was asked to talk to members of one congregation about the need to change the way they approached ministry. The pastor was concerned that within five years the church would close if it did not do something different. People were responding well until I mentioned that if they did begin to do some things differently, some people might leave the church, and they would have to be willing to let that happen. A member spoke up and said that she did not see anyone there that day she would be willing to give up. I was not surprised when that church decided not to proceed with the changes they would need to make. I was also not surprised when the pastor resigned several months later to accept another pastorate.[1]

Family needs sometimes are an indicator that it is time to move. Increasingly, we see middle-aged adult children having to move closer to aging parents to help care for them. Scripture teaches us that we are to honor our parents, and this does not stop when we grow up and move out of the home. One way to honor parents is to care for them when they begin to require some assistance. God may use the need to care for family members as one way to show us it is time to move to another place of service.

Education needs may be a valid reason to consider moving to another church. Some ministers begin their ministry, as I did, without any formal education beyond high school. A minister may realize later that a seminary education would benefit his or her ministry but finds there are no seminaries nearby. Some ministers have earned their master's degrees but feel led to pursue doctorates. Many accredited colleges and seminaries now offer online programs or weeklong intensive classes on campus that do not require students to leave their place of ministry, and most doctoral programs only require students to be on campus for a week or two at a time. However, these programs may not be suitable for every person, and the minister may feel he or she needs to move closer to the school and so must find a new church in which to minister.

Sometimes a church needs someone with different gifts and abilities than that of the current minister in order to move to a new level of ministry. This is especially true if the minister has served in the church for an extended period. Churches need different pastoral gifts for different stages of their lives. I know some ministers who are very gifted in bringing healing to a hurting church. However, once these churches become healthier, these pastors struggle to lead them in other areas of church life or ministry. A wise minister understands when he or she has taken a congregation as far as he or she can and is willing to step aside so God can bring in another minister with different gifts to lead them in new ministries.

Finances can be a valid reason to seek a new place of service. If the church cannot or will not provide a salary and benefit package that meets the needs of a minister's family, God may very well lead that minister to a new church that will be able to do so. Some will be critical of a minister leaving a church for more money and may admonish the minister to trust in the Lord to provide. I believe that God will provide, but his provision may be by way of another church that can pay a sufficient salary to meet the family's financial needs.

Clearly some ministers never unpack their boxes. They are constantly on the lookout for a church that will pay them a larger salary, provide more perks, and give them more esteem in the eyes of their peers. Almost as soon as they start work in a new church, they are looking to see which larger churches will soon open up. Such persons are hirelings (see John 10:12-13) who care nothing about the churches they serve. They care only about themselves. They fleece the sheep but never feed them. Such persons God will judge.

I am not referring to hirelings when I mention that financial considerations can be a sign God is leading a minister to another place of service. Hirelings will never be satisfied. But the ministers I am referring to take seriously the call of God on their lives, earnestly care for the people God gives them, and yet struggle to adequately provide for their families. Such people should never feel guilty if God opens up new opportunities of ministry that will financially meet the needs of their families.

Sometimes when a minister is getting closer to retirement age, he or she may need to think about moving to a smaller church, especially if health issues are beginning to occur. Some pastors want to hang on until retirement even though they know they are no longer able to adequately lead their churches. A pastor who was in a stressful ministry did not want to take early retirement but felt that remaining in his present place of ministry would be harmful to his health. He was able to find a smaller church in a nearby community that called him as pastor. He now uses his years of experience to provide a quality of leadership this church has not had in recent years, and he is mentoring a young person in the congregation who feels called to ministry. This has proven to be an excellent move for both the minister and the church, and I believe it was orchestrated by God.

We must also admit that some churches do not deserve a minister. Many churches may be difficult to lead, but others are just mean. They are mean to their ministers, the ministers' families, and to one another. If a minister chooses to stay in such an environment, he or she runs the risk of being destroyed. At the very least, such churches create much unnecessary stress in a minister's family. As soon as a minister realizes he or she is serving in a place like this, it is time to seek a new place to serve.

Steps to Making a Good Move

Once a minister is convinced that God is leading him or her to a new place of service, the next steps depend a great deal on the polity of the denomination. Some denominations leave seeking a new place of service up to the individual minister. In such cases the minister needs to let friends and colleagues know that he or she is interested in moving. The minister should ask them to share his or her name or résumé with churches they know are seeking new ministers. Other denominations, such as the one in which I serve, offer much assistance to their churches seeking new pastors and to pastors seeking new places to serve. Not everyone accepts that assistance, but those who do can expect to receive a lot of attention during the search process.

Many ministers now use Internet Web sites to get information on churches looking for new ministers. This is a fast growing phenomenon that is likely to be even more common in the future. There are risks to both churches and individuals who use these sites, and checking as many references as possible becomes even more important. However, some very good matches have occurred between churches and ministers who use this method, which means that it will probably be even more popular in the future.

Eventually, a church search committee will contact the minister, and the actions of each after this contact will largely determine the success of the process. The steps will vary somewhat by denomination, and even between churches, but the following example depicts what many Protestant ministers will experience.

Often the search committee, especially if the church is distant from the minister's current residence, will want an initial telephone interview. This is just to determine if both parties have an interest in moving forward. If interest does exist, an interview will be set up. This is a time of great stress for many ministers and their families. The minister does not know what questions the committee will ask, nor does he or she usually know yet what congregation members are looking for in their next minister. The minister is also concerned about what questions he or she needs to ask the committee.

My experience has been that many search committees do not know what to ask their candidates, and in too many cases they end up knowing little more about the person after the interview than they did before it. The danger here is that since both sides are courting each other, they may be less willing to be as honest as they should be. Years ago I read of a pastor who went to a new church with great enthusiasm only to learn the following soon after arriving:

- The previous pastor had not left for another church but had resigned when someone discovered he had been involved in an adulterous affair.
- A mortgage payment of eleven thousand dollars was due in a month or the church would lose its building.
- The church was deeply in debt because of a building program led by the previous pastor, and that debt included a balloon payment of two hundred and thirty-five thousand dollars due in two years that no one in the church knew about.[2]

If that pastor had stress about whether or not to make a move, imagine the stress he felt after he learned about the problems he had inherited. Honest, open discussions between the church and the prospective new minister can help prevent these types of things from happening. If a committee does not know what to ask or tell the minister during the interview process, the minister better have a good list of questions to ask the committee. In a previous book I shared a list of the questions that I have asked search committees during interviews so I could learn as much about that church as possible.[3] More than one committee later told me that my questions made them think and helped them prepare for other interviews with other candidates.

Many committees request an audio or video of one or more sermons the minister has delivered. Some ask for an entire worship service to see how the minister leads the service. In the past, committees would usually attend a worship service to observe the minister and see how he or she interacted with the congregation during the service and message. This normally created a great deal of stress in the church, unless it was a very large church, because the congregation members could tell that this group of visitors was a search committee with an interest in their pastor. Today, many search committees will ask that the minister preach at a neutral site to eliminate this stress for the church. This can save the minister from having to answer many embarrassing questions from people who want to know why he or she wants to leave them.

Assuming the search committee interviews go well and the committee members like the sermons they hear, the committee may schedule a candidating weekend so the minister and family can see the community and meet the congregation. A trial sermon will usually be scheduled for that Sunday morning with a congregational vote taken according to the church's constitution. A minister should take this opportunity to schedule meetings with the leadership board and other staff persons in the church. This can give the minister time to get other people's perspectives on what the church is seeking in a pastor and to talk to those with whom he or she will be working most closely.

Often a meal is scheduled that includes time for the church members to ask questions of the prospective minister. This is a time for the minister to honestly let the people learn about his or her core values and beliefs about ministry. Although a minister wants to make a positive impression, he or she does not want to mislead people to be called to the church. Such misrepresentation will only create problems later. Listening to the questions from the people will tell the minister what they want from their next pastor. The minister should also be willing to tell them what he or she expects from the congregation. Clearly, the minister will be speaking in generalities because he or she does not yet know the congregation members nor their gifts and passions. But this is an excellent time for a minister to let the congregation members know what he or she is looking for in a church before they issue a call.

Before the candidating weekend a minister and his or her family must agree that the minister will accept the position if the congregation votes accordingly. If the minister or any family members have doubts or questions, the minister should not agree to the weekend or the trial sermon. One church recently had a candidating weekend with a minister that resulted in a unanimous call from the church. The minister declined, citing family concerns about moving. The congregation members were understandably upset, because they had spent much time, energy, and expense to interview this person and bring him and his family to the community, not once but twice. The problem was that the family had never reached an agreement about making the move, and the minister had taken the church to this stage without family approval. A minister and family should agree on their willingness to accept a church's call, if offered, before consenting to a candidating weekend.

This means that all matters concerning the responsibilities of the position, the salary and benefit package, and everything else related to the position have been discussed and agreed to. The candidating weekend is not the time to reopen negotiations. The search committee, the minister, and his or her family should have a clear understanding of everything in the agreement. If anything needs congregational approval, such approval should be obtained prior to the candidating weekend. The congregation members of one church traditionally offered their pastors two weeks vacation. As they interviewed an experienced minister, he asked for four weeks vacation since he was receiving that in his present church. The committee members felt they needed congregational approval before agreeing to it, which they received at their next business meeting. When the minister was ready to be presented to the church, the minister and the search committee were in agreement about what had been offered, and the congregation members had already agreed to the negotiated changes in their minister's benefit package.

The search process is a stressful time for the minister and family, but understanding the process and having a plan for each step of the process can help reduce some of that stress. Remembering to let God be in charge also helps. God will sometimes open and close doors of ministry opportunities for reasons we may not understand. If we try to bypass God in this process, we run a greater risk of making a bad move.

Who Can Help a Minister with This Decision?

Because a decision to move affects ministers' families, they must be involved right from the beginning. If the spouse works outside the home, a move will certainly have an impact on him or her. Sometimes children are reluctant to move if they are nearing graduation from high school. They don't want to leave their friends and move to a new school system, especially if they have been in their current school for a number of years. A move at this time can be very upsetting to them.

Some people would argue that if God is leading a minister to a new church, then family considerations should not apply. These people would say that the only thing that matters in such situations is doing the will of God. In my opinion, this is a very shortsighted view of how

God leads people and makes his will known. I find that God most often leads people through the circumstances of their lives.

I have written elsewhere of the commitment I made to our son that we would not move until he completed high school.[4] This became a concern of his during his sophomore year. When we learned of his concern, my wife and I prayed for several days before sensing that God was leading us to make this commitment to him. At the time I was a bivocational pastor with a second job that would provide for all our physical needs. Even if our church asked me to resign, it would have little impact on our financial situation. We felt very comfortable making this commitment, and it had a positive effect on our son.

It is a tragic mistake for ministers to not include their families in this decision, but ministers also need to seek the counsel of other godly people. As a judicatory leader I often receive calls from ministers who want to talk about making a change in their ministries. Sometimes after we talk, they decide to stay where they are, and at other times they become open to a move. When I was a pastor thinking about making a move, I contacted my area minister to discuss it with him. A few days later we played a round of golf while we talked about ministry options that might be open to me. Some of the options he mentioned I had never considered before our conversation. I had been limiting what God might want to do with my ministry and would have continued limiting myself if I had not sought his counsel. Only a few years after that conversation, I did make a move, and interestingly enough, it was to accept the position he was leaving as he made a ministry move himself.

However, regardless of whose counsel a minister seeks, the decision to make a ministry move, as observed earlier, is one the minister alone must make. It is a decision that requires much prayer and time alone with God. There are many things to consider, and the minister will need God's help to sort them all out.

How Does a Minister Tell the Current Congregation?

This was the question that almost made me refuse the offer to become an area minister. I had served the members of this congregation for two decades and truly loved them. We were in the midst of building a new fellowship hall. Things were going well in the church. Every time I thought about having to tell them I was leaving, I wanted to reverse my decision to avoid the pain. However, I knew that God had opened up this opportunity, and I believed the church needed new leadership with different gifts than I had to lead them to a new level of ministry.

Because I was going into a judicatory ministry, I did not have to be concerned about a church vote. Our regional board would vote on the recommendation by our personnel committee about calling me. Prior to the vote, I visited our deacons individually to tell them my decision to accept the position if it was offered. There were tears during those conversations. Two weeks later the regional board approved the recommendation to call me, and the following Sunday I announced it to the church.

In many Baptist churches such an announcement is made after the sermon is preached and the invitational hymn is sung. The minister asks everyone to sit back down and then announces his or her decision to leave the church. In my opinion, that sermon is wasted because everyone will only remember the resignation at the end of the service. I made my announcement as the main focus of my sermon. This gave me time to explain my reasons for my decision and the next steps for the church. Our constitution called for four weeks notice by the minister, but I asked for six weeks so I could preach a sermon series I prepared to help with the transition the church was facing. During the next six weeks there were many joys remembered and many tears shared, but it was a healthy closing to a good ministry.

The Pressure of Having to Move

Trying to decide whether or not to change ministries is stressful enough, but when the minister is forced to look for a new place to serve, the stress is even greater. Ministers are being terminated by their churches at an alarming rate. In the Southern Baptist Convention alone there were 1,302 clergy dismissed from their churches in 2005.[5] This does not take into account the number forced to resign. All these terminations and resignations mean there are many families experiencing a great amount of stress, and this is just from one denomination.

During such times panic can easily enter the picture. How will the minister provide for his or her family? If the minister lives in a parsonage, where will his or her family live? Self-esteem issues come into play as well. It is easy for a minister to feel like a failure and wonder how things could have gone so wrong.

If a minister's church is part of a denomination, he or she needs to contact the judicatory minister as soon as possible. Hopefully, the minister has already been in dialogue with him or her about the problems in the church. Seldom does a termination come completely unexpected. It is likely there have been issues brewing for some time, and the judicatory minister should have been involved in trying to resolve them. A minister should let the judicatory leader know that he or she must find a new place of service as quickly as possible. The judicatory minister may even be able to advocate for a fair severance package to ensure the minister's family has some means of support for a few months after leaving the church.

This may be a good time for a minister to meet with a ministry evaluation center such as the Midwest Ministry Development or the Southwest Ministry Development, especially if this is not the first time he or she has encountered major problems in the ministry. These centers assist ministers needing vocational guidance during times of transition or when something seems to be lacking in their ministries. Several denominations partner with these centers, though anyone may use their services. With offices located throughout the Midwest and Southwest, they are easily accessible to many ministers.[6] Sometimes a terminating church will be willing to pay for this evaluation as part of the severance package. A minister may also want to take the opportunity to talk to a third party about his or her feelings during this difficult time in life. A minister's spouse should take advantage of this ministry as well.

Being forced out of a ministry position is one of the most stress-filled times a minister and family will experience. So many spiritual, economic, and emotional factors come into play during these times that a minister should not go through them alone. He or she should be around friends and family with their love, support, and encouragement. A minister should allow ministry colleagues to minister to him or her as well. Many ministers have probably ministered to others for so long that being on the receiving end may be uncomfortable, but they should allow God to minister to their pain and confusion through those he will bring into their lives.

Finding a new place to serve is always a difficult time. It is impossible to eliminate all the stresses that occur during such transitions, but by following the steps outlined in this chapter a minister can experience a reduction in stress. Above all, he or she must trust God in finding a place to serve, whether it is to a first pastorate or a move to a new place of ministry. Friends and judicatory leaders can assist in this transition. Such an occasion is an opportunity for the minister to deepen his or her relationship with God through increased time spent in prayer and greater attention given to God's direction for life and ministry.

Pressures of Leadership

Persons spend three years in seminary earning a master's degree that will prepare them to serve as ministers in local churches. While in seminary they are taught how to translate the Scriptures from the Greek and Hebrew texts. They learn about church history. They take classes in Old and New Testament studies, theology, hermeneutics, and ethics. The students receive instruction in preaching and leading worship services. All of these things are helpful for a minister to know, and most will be useful during his or her ministry. The problem is that although most members of a congregation want their ministers to be knowledgeable about such things, these are not the topics or tasks most ministers will be asked to know or perform in their churches.

New ministers arrive at their first churches with a library filled with books on biblical languages, archeology, systematic theology, and biblical and church history only to find that the congregation wants them to help a young couple on the verge of divorce, resolve a ten-year-old dispute between two of the deacons, and help a church member who is in jail again for drunk driving. Along with all that, ministers are to preach terrific messages three times a week, lead the church in dynamic and exciting growth, and model for the church and community how to have a happy, perfect family.

After six months in a church, young ministers wonder how they missed that many classes in seminary, because they just can't remember any courses that addressed the things the church is asking them to handle. The problem is that they didn't miss those classes; in many cases the classes were never offered. While the seminary was training them to be good research theologians, the church was looking for leaders. Daniel Aleshire, executive director of the Association of Theological Schools, acknowledges the problem. During a 2003 workshop, he presented a paper that said,

Another aspect of front line seminaries involves far more consideration about what it means to educate leaders. At its best, theological education is leadership education. Most of the M.Div. graduates of ATS schools will go into first jobs after seminary that entail a significant degree of leadership. We know that failures in early ministry careers are not typically related to defective knowledge of scripture or church history, but are most typically a function of relational problems or inadequate abilities as leaders. Leadership is good work, and when it is done well, it helps a community to accomplish the purposes and goals that only a company of persons working together can accomplish. I think theological education needs a more inclusive perspective about ministerial leadership, and the educational imagination and skill to educate effectively toward that perspective.[1]

Fortunately, some seminaries are now offering classes in leadership and giving their students some of the practical skills they will need to serve their churches. Liberty Theological Seminary now has a leadership track in their master of arts in religion program. Students who choose this track will take five courses in different aspects of leadership. Some schools require leadership courses as part of their studies, while others offer such courses as electives.

However, just because seminaries are now offering leadership courses does not mean ministers are comfortable in that role. In fact, many are not even sure what leadership means. Walk into any bookstore, secular or Christian, and you will find a plethora of books on leadership, each giving its description of what a leader does. Is the minister called to be a servant leader or to function as a CEO? In some churches, especially smaller ones, will the minister ever be the leader or would it be wiser for him or her to identify the true leaders in the church and work through them to accomplish ministry? Do some churches need a Jack Welch* type of leader, while others require a Mother Teresa style of leadership? The same leadership style will not work in every church, and ministers must adapt their styles to the particular dynamics and needs of the places they currently serve. This requires wisdom and time to get to know the congregation. With so

---

*Former CEO and chairman of General Electric

many questions surrounding leadership, it is no wonder that many ministers feel pressure when asked to provide it.

Reducing the Leadership Pressures

Every church is different, and any minister who believes that his or her leadership style can simply be transferred from one church to another is mistaken. A smaller church usually has patriarchs or matriarchs who have provided leadership in that church for years. They have seen numerous ministers come and go, but they were the ones who stayed faithful to the church and saw it through its good and bad times. They will not yield their influence in that church lightly. A minister will normally have to serve a smaller church for an extended period before being accepted as a leader in that church. Prior to that, the most effective way to exercise leadership is to work through the already established leaders.

Ministers should make the lay leaders their allies in the changes they want to make. They should run their ideas by those leaders before taking them to the congregation. Lay leaders may point out some reasons why the church is not ready for the proposed changes. Shortly after beginning my pastorate our church had a business meeting. My only proposal in that meeting was soundly rejected by nearly everyone in attendance. Later that evening a member phoned me and explained that my recommendation had brought up some very painful memories of something similar that was tried several years earlier. I was too new at the church to know its history, and unknowingly, I had stepped on a land mine in that congregation. If I had shared my thoughts with some of the lay leaders before the business meeting, they would have explained why this was not a good time for my plan.

If lay leaders believe a minister's ideas have merit, they will often present them to the church, and the minister can be almost certain they will be accepted. The congregation already recognizes these people as leaders, and if the leaders think something is a good idea, it is likely others will as well.

Leadership in Medium-Sized Churches

When a minister moves from a family church (less than 50 active members) to a pastoral church (50 to 150 active members), the leadership needs usually change. Pastors of family churches, which are often led by strong patriarchs and/or matriarchs, may be no more than chaplains, especially at first. Moving to a pastoral church will place the pastor at the center of most activities. Pastors of these churches must have strong leadership gifts and be able to communicate and delegate well.

Leadership changes required from such a move will also depend on the prior experiences of the church. Members of a congregation with a history of strong pastoral leadership will expect that same style from their new pastor. If congregation members have operated with a consensus style of leadership, they will also expect to continue to make decisions by consensus. What does not vary in a church of this size is vision, which becomes an important component of leadership.

My favorite definition of vision comes from George Barna: "Vision for ministry is a clear mental image of a preferable future imparted by God to His chosen servants and is based upon an accurate understanding of God, self and circumstances."[2] It is impossible to lead a church into "a preferable future" unless one has first seen a glimpse of what that future looks like. The first challenge for the leader is to discern God's vision for the church, and the second challenge is to communicate that vision so clearly that the congregation members buy into it. Unless they own the vision, it is unlikely it will ever come to pass.

Different styles of leadership impact vision in different ways. Barna describes four types of leaders. The first is the directing leader, who is great at communicating a compelling vision to the church and creating a great deal of energy around that vision. Such leaders are not good with the details of achieving the vision and need other people to work those details out.

A second style of leadership is the strategic leader, who is best at shaping the vision. These leaders gather the information needed to make the vision possible. They tend to move slowly because they want to acquire as much information as possible before making any decisions.

The team-building leader is gifted at bringing the congregation together to achieve the vision. They believe that each person has a part in seeing the vision accomplished, and they excel in encouraging others to find a role in that effort.

The final leader Barna identifies is the operational leader, who is able to develop the systems required to achieve the vision. They make the process run smoothly so there is a minimal amount of chaos and conflict around the vision.[3]

A minister must first identify which style best represents him or her and then bring in other people who can compensate for the weaknesses that exist in that style. Few leaders are able to effectively handle all aspects of identifying a vision and leading the church to achieve it. Teamwork becomes essential. John Maxwell correctly observes that "one is too small a number to achieve greatness."[4] Leaders recognize that they need to bring others on board if they want to accomplish anything of significance in their churches.

Leadership in Larger Churches

The minister is expected to provide a different level of leadership in the larger churches. The minister will work directly with few in the congregation except for those in leadership positions. Team leadership becomes a necessity in the larger churches. The minister will provide vision and leadership to the leaders of the different departments within the church, who, in turn, will direct and lead those departments. It is in this size church that the CEO model of leadership is most effective.

Not every minister is able to provide this type of leadership. Some are committed to a shepherding ministry that will be ineffective in the larger churches. Others do not have the gifts or the temperament for such leadership. Before accepting a call to a larger church a minister must be certain he or she is comfortable providing this type of leadership. If a person is considering such a call, he or she should visit a ministry evaluation center (see chapter 3) to have his or her leadership gifts evaluated to determine if they will work well in a larger ministry setting.

What we have seen so far in this chapter is that there are different types of acceptable leadership styles that will fit in different churches and in different situations. There is no one right approach to leadership in ministry settings. One minister's leadership style may be very different from the style of another in the community, and yet both can be equally effective. This should be great news to those who are reluctant to view themselves as leaders.

Reluctant Leaders

Because of some misconceptions about the nature of leadership many ministers are reluctant to identify themselves as leaders. They do not see themselves as the John Wayne or George Patton types, and those are the models that first come to some people's minds when they think of leaders. However, that is only one model of leadership. If we recognize that leading is a matter of influence, then we can create an entirely different understanding of leadership.[5] Being a leader does not mean accomplishing objectives no matter what the human cost. Being a leader means influencing others to work together to achieve the objectives God has set before his church.

As we continue into the twenty-first century, we will find the forceful, take-no-prisoners style of leadership to be ineffective in the church and marketplace. "Effective leadership will be concerned both with producing high-quality results and with promoting a healthy, graceful, and stimulating work environment."[6] Such leadership will be as concerned with the well-being of the people being led as with achieving tasks. One sign that leadership is moving in this direction is the rediscovery by many of the classic book written by Robert Greenleaf, *Servant Leadership*, in which he insists that "the servant-leader *is* servant first."[7] Servant leaders will lead their people to the fulfillment of the mission God has given them, but they will not sacrifice those people to achieve the mission.

Even with this improved way of understanding leadership some ministers are still reluctant to view themselves as leaders. Actually, that is not always a bad thing. A few years before I entered pastoral ministry, I watched two men campaign for an open spot on our church's board of deacons. One of our deacons had moved, and the position would be filled with an election. I knew both men well, and I became very disappointed in each of them. The only things that were missing were yard signs and political ads in the church newsletter. I had never seen two people work so hard for a volunteer position. They put our church in a difficult position because one of these men was going to lose the election, and I feared it would create hard feelings in the church. In the years since, I have realized that some of the best leaders in a church are often those who do not want to be leaders. A. W. Tozer noticed this as well:

A true and safe leader is likely to be one who has no desire to lead, but is forced into a position of leadership by the inward pressure of the Holy Spirit and the press of the external situation. Such were Moses and David and the Old Testament prophets. I think there was hardly a great leader from Paul to the present day but that was drafted by the Holy Spirit for the task, and commissioned by the

Lord of the Church to fill a position he had little heart for. I believe it might be accepted as a fairly reliable rule of thumb that the man who is ambitious to lead is disqualified as a leader. The true leader will have no desire to lord it over God's heritage, but will be humble, gentle, self-sacrificing and altogether as ready to follow as to lead, when the Spirit makes it clear that a wiser and more gifted man than himself has appeared.[8]

Another misconception about leadership is that leaders are born with the gifts and abilities to be leaders, and those who believe they were not born with such gifts are reluctant to take on the mantle of leadership. While it is true that some people are born with greater natural gifts of leadership, anyone can learn to be a leader. Leadership involves a number of skills nearly all of which can be learned in time.[9] If a person is already a good leader, by improving these skills he or she can become a better leader.

If a minister struggles with the idea of being a leader, there are a number of excellent books available to help improve his or her leadership skills. The important thing to remember is that if God has called a person into the ministry, that person has no choice but to be a leader. Leadership is expected of everyone God calls to serve him. We only have to look at the many churches drifting along without purpose and direction to realize that those who God called to lead them are not fulfilling that mandate.

Rather than allowing the responsibility of leadership to create stress, ministers can take comfort that there are many ways to lead. There is more than just one style of effective leadership, and God has equipped each person with just the right style. If a minister feels weak in some areas of leadership, he or she can find hope by learning how to improve in those areas. As a minister uses his or her God-given style of leadership and learns how to be a more effective leader, that minister will find an increase in his or her ability to influence others and in the production of good fruit. That will also reduce much of the stress of leadership.

Spiritual Leadership

Not only is the church leader called to be a servant leader, but he or she is also called to be a spiritual leader. Leadership should flow out of who a person is, not what a person does or the position he or she holds in the church. A person's deepening relationship with God is where he or she finds the authority to serve as a leader. The disciplines that lead to that deepening relationship are where a person hears the still, small voice of God giving him or her direction about where to lead. Once a person realizes this, it should help alleviate much of the pressure he or she feels as a leader.

5
Pressures of Preaching and Teaching

Many pastors experience a great deal of stress surrounding their preaching and teaching responsibilities. Although a number of churches are moving away from two services on Sunday and a midweek Bible study, many still have that schedule. That usually means the solo minister is responsible for three messages every week regardless of anything else that might be going on. Some have other teaching responsibilities in the church as well, such as a pastor's Sunday school class or a new member's class. Add it all up and ministers may be expected to prepare and deliver as many as one hundred and fifty to two hundred sermons and lessons each year. This is on top of all other ministerial responsibilities.

Every minister is also well aware that each time he or she speaks, people will be evaluating his or her efforts. It's no wonder that many ministers feel the pressure each week as they prepare and deliver their messages. It also explains why some ministers change churches every two or three years. It's easier to take their already prepared sermons to another church than to do the hard work of preparing new ones every week.

Ministers who take their calling seriously do not fear human critics as much as they fear God's judgment upon their efforts. James 3:1 still reads, "My brethren, let not many of you become teachers, knowing that we shall receive a stricter judgment." In the introduction to his book *Rediscovering Expository Preaching* John MacArthur Jr. writes, "No profession has as high a liability potential as that of the preacher of God's Word. God will judge every preacher on the truthfulness and accuracy of his preaching. Any failure as a spokesman for God brings not only shame (2 Tim. 2:15) but judgment."[1]

Being called to handle God's Word is no light thing. Those who have been called by God into the ministry have the awesome responsibility to study God's Word so they can proclaim its truths and principles in a way that will make a difference in people's lives. They are not called just to give a theologically or historically sound dissertation; they are called to teach God's truths so that people can understand them and apply them. I felt the burden of this responsibility every week as a pastor, but this was a part of my ministry in which I felt very little pressure, especially when I approached it with much planning and prayer.

Reducing the Preaching and Teaching Pressures

Ministry is difficult work with numerous responsibilities that demand time and energy. There are people in the hospitals to visit, people who need counseling, weddings and funerals to perform, meetings to attend, planning to be done, and a host of other activities that vary from week to week. In the midst of all this activity, there are sermons and lessons that must be prepared.

In my first semester at Bible school I learned a valuable lesson. One instructor did not give tests. He required three papers over the course of the semester, which he explained in the first class session. He also explained very clearly that any paper not turned in on the due date would automatically receive a failing grade. As good students are supposed to do, we all complained that emergencies could arise and that he surely would take those into consideration. He responded that we had the due dates in our hands, and if we waited until the last minute to write the papers, it would not be his fault. He emphasized again that he would take no emergency into consideration. We either turned the papers in on the day they were due or failed the course.

He then explained his reasons for taking this approach. Most of us were preparing to be pastors, and every week our congregations would expect a sermon from us. He reminded us that they would not care how busy we had been the previous week; they came to hear a message from the Word of God. We couldn't just walk into the pulpit; throw up our hands, and say, "Sorry, but I was too busy to prepare a sermon for today. I'll try to have something ready for next week." This meant that no matter how busy our week was, we had an obligation to our congregation and to God to be prepared when we stepped into the pulpit. We knew in advance that at the end of every busy week there would be another Sunday, and as pastors we had to be prepared for that Sunday. If we waited until we had the time to prepare our sermons, we would probably be doing a lot of "Saturday night specials" and going into the pulpit the following morning unprepared with a message that would reflect the effort we gave it.

That instructor taught me the value of planning and working ahead, and it was a practice I needed in a twenty-year bivocational pastorate. He was also one of the best instructors I had at that school, and I took every class he taught.

Sermon Planning

The most effective sermon planning comes after the minister has been at a church long enough to understand the needs of the people and to understand where God is leading the church. This requires spending much time with the members of the congregation, getting to know them and their families well. It also calls for a great deal of prayer and discernment. What are their fears, their hopes, and their dreams? Where have they been broken in the past? We have to give them time to tell us their stories and then listen closely to the stories within the stories.

We see an excellent example of this in John 4 when Jesus has a dialogue with the Samaritan woman. He encounters this woman as she comes to the well to draw water. During their conversation Jesus keeps listening to the stories the woman tells him, and each time he takes her into the story behind the story. The encounter begins innocently enough with a discussion about water, but it soon changes as the woman realizes that Jesus is offering her water that will satisfy the spiritual thirst she has. He then leads her to recognize the emptiness of her life that led her from one man to another. When she tries to avoid that conversation by asking religious questions about worship, Jesus answers the question she did not ask by telling her that he was the promised Messiah. This encounter leads not only to her salvation but also to the salvation of many of the people in her village.

One of the main complaints unchurched people have about the church is that it is no longer relevant. They complain that the church is answering questions that no one is asking, and they are often right. Until the church engages people in conversation and listens to their stories, it doesn't know what questions to answer. This is true not only of unchurched people but also of the people already in churches. Too often ministers are not spending enough time getting to know their people and their deepest needs. Until they do so they will be unable to plan their sermons to speak to those needs.

Some people will object to creating a preaching plan in advance. They argue that sermon preparation should depend on God. In fact, some insist that they do not prepare sermons but just preach whatever God gives them when they step into the pulpit. Actually, they don't need to be insistent about anything, because their lack of preparation is usually obvious. It is a shame that they blame God for what they preach! If I can believe that God will lead me when I step into the pulpit—and I do—then why is it so difficult to believe that God can lead my planning several months in advance? Is he not the omniscient God who knows all things? Does he not know what messages our churches will need to hear in the future, or does he just work from week to week?

When ministers plan their preaching in advance, they benefit in several ways. First, they do not have to spend part of the week wondering what they will preach next Sunday. They've already determined that, so they can spend that time actually preparing the sermon. That saves a lot of time. It gives them a chance to watch for illustrations and other material that will make the message better. Many ministers will keep a file folder for each sermon, and when they find something they think will fit a message, they put it in the proper folder. This practice saves even more time because they are not spending time looking for resources.

Planning also benefits the worship leaders. When the worship team knows in advance what a minister will be preaching, they can design the worship service around the theme of the message. This can improve the flow of the worship experience by putting together congregational singing, special music, drama, and visual displays that help connect people to the message.

There are many ways to develop a preaching plan. In this chapter I'll share what I did for many years. Each fall I would invest a few days creating my preaching plan for the next year. I would take sheets of paper and write the dates of each Sunday of the coming year in the left-hand margin. If that Sunday was a holiday or special occasion, I would note that to the left of the date. Because our church had two services, on Sunday I would write in AM and PM.

There were some things I did every year that I would go ahead and list on the planning sheets. The first sermon each year focused on the church's vision and emphasis for the upcoming year. Between Mother's Day and Father's Day I always preached a series of sermons that addressed family issues. The Advent and Lenten seasons were also set aside for a special series of messages built around those themes. I often preached through a book of the Bible during the summer months, and most years I knew which book I would cover well in advance so I could begin purchasing commentaries and other helps to enable me to better understand that book. Those Sundays would be reserved.

Once I had marked each of these Sundays off, I could begin working on the remaining Sundays. Sometimes there would be a Sunday by itself between those already scheduled, and I would often save it for a while in case there was a particular topic I would need to address. If there were several Sundays in a row, I would think about a possible sermon series that could be preached during those Sundays.

Some ministers who plan their sermons in advance believe they should have their sermon titles and themes planned a year ahead as well. Except for the special Sundays I've described above, I usually worked on such matters a quarter in advance. I tried to give my sermon themes to our worship leaders a month early, so sometimes I would wait until then to decide on a topic for a single Sunday. That provided me some flexibility in case I needed to address some topic in particular.

All my sermon titles and texts were written on the planning sheets in pencil to allow flexibility if something important came up. I know one minister who planned his sermons well in advance, and he would not deviate from his planned preaching schedule. The Sunday after 9/11 he preached the message he had planned months before. His congregation members complained that except for mentioning the disaster during their prayer time, no one in the church would have had any idea that anything significant had happened that week. Like many churches, they had new people attend the worship service that Sunday hoping to hear some word from God that would help renew their hope, but they were disappointed because the minister was a slave to his planning.

Sermon Preparation

Senior professor of Christian Preaching at the Southern Baptist Theological Seminary, James Cox, writes that "the integrity of the pulpit demands a lifetime study program."[2] This includes not only reading books and attending classes but also studying life and contemporary culture. Everything the minister absorbs in his or her life will come out in his or her preaching.

Still there comes a time when the minister must sit down in his or her study and begin the hard work of putting together a message for the upcoming Sunday service. If the proper planning has been done, time does not have to be spent trying to decide what to preach next Sunday. The minister can focus on preparing the actual sermon itself. There are many excellent books on how to craft a sermon, so we will not cover that ground here.

We will discuss the minister's library, however. A good library can remove much stress from sermon preparation. When I prepared my sermons, I would first read the text in different translations and think through what it was saying to me. I would then gather my commentaries to study what others found in the text. Next I would look up the sermon theme in my filing system to see what other books in my library said about the theme or text or to find illustrations that were applicable to the message. I would then be ready to start putting the sermon together.

The key was having a good library and a good filing system so I could quickly put my hands on information I needed for the sermon. The alternative was to spend hours trying to find material that I remembered seeing in a book or magazine but couldn't remember which one. For many themes I might address in a sermon, I can click on a folder on my computer and pull up pages of quotes and facts with book titles and page numbers of the sources for where I can find that information. It does take time to record these details in the system, but that time is well worth the investment when that information is later needed for sermon or lesson preparation.

Young ministers starting out do not have much money for a library, but I would encourage every minister to view his or her library as a lifelong investment in ministry. Many churches designate an amount of money each year for the pastor to purchase books and subscriptions. Some ministers use the honorariums they receive for weddings and funerals to purchase resources for their libraries. A minister should spend money wisely and purchase the resources that will add value to his or her ministry.

Ministers can save significant money by purchasing study materials that they can download into their computers. Excellent Bible study programs available on CD-ROM are much less expensive than the same material found in books. These programs combine a number of Bible translations, commentaries, books, maps, and other study aids to assist the minister in sermon preparation. Simply searching for a text or a theme will usually produce more information than anyone could possibly use in one message, and that information is accessible within a few seconds. This can considerably reduce the time needed for sermon preparation.

Ministers should be aware of one thing before buying any Bible study software. They must know what they are buying before making the purchase. Some of these programs are very technical and are probably better suited for a student working on a PhD in biblical languages. Other programs, especially the least expensive ones, often provide very outdated Bible study materials. Neither of these programs will offer much help to a minister wanting to speak to a twenty-first-century congregation. Trying to use these programs will likely create even more stress.

Public and school libraries continue to be free. If a minister lives close to a seminary or college with a good library, he or she can often go there for a few hours of study and access to more resources than he or she could ever purchase. The trade-off is that it may not be convenient. Many of these libraries permit outside persons to purchase library cards at a very reasonable cost. I have a card that only cost me ten dollars, but it allows me to check out books from a local college. The college library is on the Internet, so if I am looking for a particular book, I can check the library site and know within a few minutes whether the library carries it and if it is available.

Relating the Message to the Audience

All the study and preparation in the world will go to waste if the minister is not able to connect his or her message with the audience. Graham Johnston describes well the challenge facing today's ministers when he writes, "Remember, twenty-first-century listeners have grown up on television with remote control units in their hands—and this is an entire generation with attention deficit disorder."[3] Ministers must engage their audiences with questions, stories, illustrations, and practical applications, as well as biblical instruction. Because we do live in a visual society, the minister must speak in a way that creates pictures in the minds of the listeners.[4]

Listeners can more easily relate to a minister who honestly admits his or her own struggles in life. At one time, ministers conducted themselves as if they were above the struggles other people experienced. People probably didn't believe that was true then, and they certainly will not believe it is true today. The media is filled with reports of ministerial struggles and failures, and these reports include nationally televised preachers as well as local ministers. Ministers wrestle with the same temptations that every other created human being does. Their families encounter the same pressures that other families in the churches have. They experience the same faith questions others face when confronted with financial, health, and relationship difficulties. The list goes on and on.

In his studies of formerly unchurched people, Thom Rainer found that one of the critical issues that led these people to faith was the transparent preaching of the minister. They were looking to see if anybody was real and willing to be honest. One pastor reported to Rainer that he felt that if he wasn't authentic in his preaching, his listeners might think that Christ is not real either.[5]

Clearly, this authenticity is an important part of connecting with listeners, but where does the minister draw the line? For many ministers, even the thought of revealing the mistakes of their past, much less the struggles of the present, would create a huge amount of stress. If ministers reveal their struggles, others may question their ability to lead a church, and there are cases in which ministers were forced to leave their churches because of past decisions they made and later shared with others.

In my own ministry I have been at both extremes. There have been times when I've guarded my life so closely that some may have wondered if I even had a life. I have deprived myself and my family of other people's prayers to keep a situation private. At other times I have been too transparent, and my openness may have disappointed some congregation members who preferred their minister to be above the problems of other mortals.

A balanced approach for the minister might be admitting that he or she has areas of struggle just like everyone else but then not go into details. Such balance protects the minister from revealing too much information but also allows the minister to be open about his or her own life. Such an approach helps congregation members see both struggles and victories in their pastor's life. If the pastor faces the same difficulties they do and God is at work transforming his or her life, then God can likewise be at work transforming theirs too.

Being willing to be transparent also helps take some of the pressure off the minister because he or she no longer has to worry about trying to live up to unrealistic expectations. More importantly, transparency in a minister's preaching allows others to see that he or she also has questions and sometimes struggles with issues of faith and that such struggles are all right.

Collaborative Preaching

One model of sermon preparation that has received attention lately is collaborative preaching. This model includes other people in the preparation of the sermon. Some ministers now find it helpful to invite a small group of people who reflect the makeup of the congregation to join them as they begin work on the message. A minister can learn what the text says to such a group and what questions it raises for them. The group may also raise questions the minister never considered in his or her study of the text.

After the message is delivered, the group meets again to evaluate its effectiveness. Few ministers receive constructive feedback of their sermons except for the comments made as people are leaving the service. It is helpful for a minister to hear from people whom he or she trusts will provide honest feedback; such feedback is essential for the minister's growth in his or her speaking responsibilities. In some churches with more than one service on Sunday morning, this feedback may occur between the services so that needed changes can be made before the next service begins.

Such collaboration does not diminish the minister's responsibility for preparing the message.[6] He or she is still responsible for doing the hard work of exegesis and for praying and seeking God's leading in the message being developed, but God may choose to do that leading through the collaboration team. There are many benefits to the minister who uses a team to assist with the sermon preparation and evaluation. One of those benefits is a reduction in the stress often associated with developing a message every week.

Does the Minister Really Have to Speak at Every Service?

Although some ministers believe they must have a fresh word from the Lord for every service, not everyone in the church may feel that way. In larger churches staff persons speak at some services, and the senior pastor may only preach thirty-five to forty times a year. In medium-sized churches there may be lay leaders who would be interested in speaking occasionally. Some of these persons may be sensing a call to the ministry, and the opportunity to deliver a message may help them know how to respond to that sense of calling.

Ministers should also make use of some of the excellent videos available today. Once or twice a year I would use a video series, usually on Sunday nights, that provided a learning opportunity that the church could not otherwise have. One popular series I used, called *That the World May Know*, featured a person who led groups through the Holy Land and pointed out details that were behind many of the lessons taught throughout the Bible. Each series lasted a few weeks, which not only gave me a brief break in my sermon preparation but also exposed our small congregation to some important archeological finds and information. Those video series were then added to the church library for small groups or families to use for further study.

The solo or senior minister in a church is ultimately responsible for the message presented to the congregation each week. However, that does not mean he or she is the only one who can speak to that congregation. There are many ways to present biblical truth to the church each week that does not require the minister to deliver every message. Nor does a minister have to be alone in his or her sermon preparation. The use of excellent commentaries, collaborative groups, and other resources can assist a minister's sermon preparation and remove some of the pressure of that preparation.

Ministers do have an awesome responsibility before God to teach sound doctrine and truth to their congregations, but it does not have to be a point of pressure in our ministries. Spending time in prayer to discern the needs of the congregation and community, careful sermon planning, and the use of excellent resources can make sermon preparation less stressful and much more enjoyable.

6
Pressures of Pastoral Care and Counseling

I began my pastoral ministry with no education beyond high school and no training in theology or practical ministry skills. After serving as a pastor for only a short time I realized I needed help in many areas but especially in the areas of pastoral care and counseling. People were seeking my advice on a wide range of issues mainly having to do with marriage and family problems. We had people going into the hospital and facing long-term medical problems. Judging from the age of the congregation, we were likely facing a number of funerals in the next few years, and at that time I had only attended one or two funerals in my life. I simply did not know how to address the many pastoral care issues that existed in our church, and this pressure was what led me to attend a small Bible school near our community.

Preaching and pastoral care are the two most important tasks of the minister, especially in small and medium-sized churches. Through the pulpit ministry the minister can shape and guide congregation members to fulfill God's purpose for their church, but through pastoral care the minister earns the right to speak. We've all heard the cliché "People don't care how much you know until they know how much you care." Ministers earn the right to speak to the people when they have spent time with them in the hospital, sat with them to discuss a wayward child, and ministered to them when they lost their jobs. Ministers also earn the right to speak when they have rejoiced with the people over the birth of a new child, the move into a new home, and the wedding of their children. It is when ministers walk through a crisis with their people that they become their people's pastor.

Ministerial ethics requires that the minister not return to his or her former church to do weddings and funerals unless the new minister specifically asks. Why is this so important? Because it is through these types of events that the new minister connects on a personal level with the congregation members. John Maxwell has identified the Law of Connection as one of the essential laws of leadership. Maxwell writes that leaders must touch a heart before they ask for a hand.[1] The way pastors connect with members of their congregations is through the pastoral care they provide.

Pastoral Care Is Time Consuming

One of the stresses associated with pastoral care is that it demands a lot of the minister's time. The minister may have members of the congregation in several area hospitals at once, funerals and weddings to conduct, and a long list of persons who need to talk. Pastoral care can easily consume every working hour and leave little time for all the other responsibilities of pastoral ministry.

Another stress is that some ministers are not especially gifted in pastoral care. Some have the gifts of mercy, helps, and healing that lend themselves to pastoral care, while others are more gifted in leadership, preaching, and administration. Ministers tend to be intuitive in the areas of their giftedness, so someone in the latter group can easily walk right past someone who is hurting and never see the need in that person's life. I tend to fall into that group, and there were times during my ministry when my wife would insist that someone in our church needed a pastoral visit because she sensed something was bothering that individual. She is strongly gifted in the area of mercy, and she can spot hurting people much quicker than I can. I learned to listen to her intuition, trust her judgment, and call on those people, and in nearly every case she was right. Those people did need a pastoral ear to listen to them.

Another stress associated with this area of ministry is that no pastor can possibly be an expert on every need. Life is complicated and getting more complicated all the time. People present ministers with a host of problems that many of them were never trained to address. Just as a medical doctor cannot be an expert in all areas of medicine, a minister cannot be an expert in all the different problems people will bring to his or her attention. Yet some in the congregation will expect just that from their pastor.

Another reality that produces stress for the minister is that some-times the problems he or she is asked to address are also problems in their own lives. As I said in an earlier chapter, ministers are not exempt from having problems in their homes. How can they assist persons in their congregations with problem marriages and difficult children without feeling like hypocrites? How can they provide financial advice when they are past due on their car payments? How can they help a person who wants to know how to forgive someone when they have a list of persons they struggle to forgive? What minister has not been in the midst of providing pastoral care to someone and found it difficult to apply the same advice to his or her own situation?

A year ago I preached in a church while the pastor was away on vacation. This church was in my hometown, so I knew many of the people who attend, and I have preached there on numerous occasions. A few weeks later a young man from the church approached me and said, "I took your advice." He then explained that in my message that Sunday I had said that each of us needs to determine God's purpose for our lives and find a way to fulfill that purpose. He went on to say that for years he wanted to start a lawn care business but was afraid to quit his job and go into business for himself. However, after hearing my message he did just that! He thanked me for giving him the courage to take a step of faith he had wanted to take for a long time.

While I was excited for him, I also knew that if this business failed, some people would blame me. That is another stress associated with pastoral care. People who follow a minister's advice will sometimes blame the minister if things don't go the way they hope.

Several years ago I was doing premarital counseling with a couple each of whom had been previously married. One of the items I stress in my sessions with couples is the importance of communication. I challenge them to talk about things they had never discussed before. On the afternoon of our next session the man called to cancel their ap-pointment for that evening. I asked when he would like to reschedule, and he replied they were no longer getting married. After our previous session they began to talk about where they would live. Each had as-sumed after they got married that they would live in the home he or she currently lived in. It turned out neither of them wanted to move from his or her home, so they decided they would not get married. I'm thankful they had that conversation before getting married or they might have had a very short honeymoon. Sometime later I heard that the man was marrying a different woman, and he had a different clergyman perform the ceremony. I guess he didn't want to take a chance on me costing him another marriage!

Some people who call on a minister for pastoral care are just seeking someone to agree with their position. If the minister happens to voice a different viewpoint, these people will reject his or her advice. They may even turn against the minister, leave the church, and tell people the minister "wasn't there for them in their time of need." This is just another pressure associated with pastoral care and counseling.

It is also possible for a minister to assist people and still lose them from the church. A pastor told me about a couple with marriage problems that he worked with almost weekly for nearly a year. During the course of their conversations both admitted to having affairs. The pastor said he was able to help them restore their marriage, but they left the church, embarrassed because of what he knew about them.

Reducing the Pressures of Pastoral Care and Counseling

One of the main ways for a minister to reduce the stress associated with providing pastoral care is to limit the amount of pastoral care he or she provides. For too long one of the pastor's main roles has been to provide pastoral care to the congregation. This is not the pastor's job according to Eph. 4:10-16. The pastor's role is to train and equip congregation members to minister to one another. We need to stop talking about pastoral care and start focusing on congregational care.[2]

Many churches today claim they want a pastor who is a leader, but the gifts they regularly look for in a pastor are the pastoral care gifts. I pointed this out once to the members of a search committee who insisted they wanted a pastor who could provide them with the strong leadership necessary to help the church have a greater impact in its community. A survey the committee conducted with the congregation showed that the church was actually seeking a chaplain who would faithfully minister to the church members. The church wanted a chaplain, not a leader. I cautioned the committee members that they would be unlikely to find a person who could lead the church in a powerful outreach to the community while spending all of his or her time visiting church members.

The nurturing ministries of a congregation entail far more than any person, no matter how gifted, can provide. Instead of the pastor conceptualizing the nurturing task as all his or her responsibility, the goal must be to mobilize the congregation to reach out in care and nurture—to each other and to needs outside their community of faith. The pastor's objective then becomes developing "ministers of care" who nurture and develop other nurturers until all members of the community of faith are equipped to reach to and care for family members, neighbors, and those in their sphere of daily interaction.[3]

This does not mean that the pastor never provides pastoral care to the congregation. It does mean the pastor is not automatically the first person called when someone in the church needs ministry. Others in the church must be trained to be first responders, and the congregation must be trained to call these persons before calling the pastor.

The Southern Baptist Convention has an excellent program called the Deacon Family Ministry Plan. I have used it as both a deacon and as a pastor. The plan is very simple to set up. Every person or family in the church is divided among the active deacons in the church. These deacons contact their families on birthdays, anniversaries, and other special occasions. They also visit their families if they go into the hospital or have other issues going on in their lives. If warranted, the deacons can contact the pastor for additional follow-up ministry with these persons. While some people expect the pastor to be the person calling on them in times of need, most will enjoy having the congregational lay leaders minister to them as well.

Some churches refer to their congregational ministry as a shepherding program. Most that I have seen have been set up similar to the program described above. Churches with small groups that meet regularly use the leaders of those groups as the primary shepherds for the persons in their groups. In every case, if the situation requires it, someone can call in the pastor to provide additional pastoral care.

These programs require a willingness from the lay leaders to provide such ministry and training. I was a deacon before becoming a pastor, and our church used the Deacon Family Ministry Plan. While most of our deacons were very conscientious, some did very little with their families. I was a member of that church for nearly two years and didn't even know which deacon was assigned to my family until I finally asked at the church office. Other deacons regularly ministered to their families in a host of different ways. I knew one deacon who expected a call from a family near the end of each month with a request for food, and he would take them a bag of groceries.

Even the most willing individual needs training to learn how to minister to members of the congregation, and the pastor's responsibility is to provide such training. A pastor can contact his or her denomination's regional or district office to learn what tools are available to make such training easier.

One of the most effective training tools is for a minister to invite others to come along when he or she is providing pastoral care. They can listen to the minister's prayers and see how the minister relates to persons with different needs. The next time the minister takes them, he or she can allow them more participation in the ministry. Soon they will be able to go alone and also help in training others. This should be part of the discipling ministry of every church so that new believers can learn how to become ministers and fulfill the calling God has on their lives.

Training the congregation to call on the lay ministers in the church instead of the pastor is often a challenge. Longtime members are probably conditioned to call on the pastor anytime they have a need. They will not easily change their habits and call on others in the church for ministry. The pastor must remind them that Gal. 6:2 says, "Bear one another's burdens, and so fulfill the law of Christ." This verse teaches that congregation members are to minister to one another.

The pastor can also remind congregation members that dividing them up among several persons trained to provide ministry means that someone will likely respond much sooner to their requests than is possible for the pastor. The pastor will also be able to respond sooner to the most urgent needs if he or she is not spending time with needs that are less pressing.

Training others to provide congregational care relieves many of the stresses associated with pastoral care. It reduces the amount of time required for pastoral care because that work is distributed among several persons and the minister is only ministering to the most serious needs. Persons should be selected for these lay ministry roles on the basis of their having suitable gifts for such a ministry. This will allow the pastor without those particular gifts to work more in the areas of his or her strengths. However, this still does not address the stress ministers have when asked to assist someone in an area where their knowledge is limited.

Assemble a Team

Serious situations usually require trained lay leaders to call their pastor; however, the pastor still does not need to be the only person ministering. A wise pastor will seek the help of a team of trusted Christian individuals who have expertise in a wide variety of fields. He or she may need to call in lawyers to help someone address legal questions or social workers in cases of abuse or neglect. A minister should have mental health professionals to whom he or she can make referrals. This doesn't mean a minister is neglecting his or her pastoral care responsibilities; it does mean he or she is committed to assisting people in finding the best help possible for their problems.

A member of our church who was a single mother once called me concerned about a diagnosis a mechanic gave her about her car. She felt he was trying to take advantage of her because she was a woman. She had little disposable income and didn't know what to do. Since I know little about automobiles, I asked her to call my mechanic and have him look at her car. I then called him, explained the situation, and told him to expect her call. When he examined her car, he found it needed only a minor repair that was much less expensive than what the first mechanic had suggested. This young mother received pastoral care from the hands of an auto mechanic who was not even a member of our church, and all it took was a phone call.

Churches often receive calls from people passing through the area who need a place to spend the night. Owners of local motels should be on the minister's pastoral care team. Discounted rates for rooms could be negotiated, saving the church money and ministering to this need. In return, the church could promise to use the motel when it has out-of-town speakers needing someplace to stay.

The list of persons a pastor can add to a pastoral care team is endless, and everyone on that list does not have to be a member of the church. It should include people who have expertise in areas in which the minister is less knowledgeable. This ensures that persons receive the best care available to them and, for the pastor, reduces the pressure of trying to minister in an area in which he or she is not really qualified.

Offer Pastoral Care to Groups

People within a congregation share many of the same pastoral care issues. Not all of these issues can be addressed in a group setting, but some of them can. In our small church I required premarital instruction before I would agree to marry a couple. I gave this instruction to individual couples, which usually required four sessions. Imagine how much time I would need if I had twenty or more weddings a year. Some larger churches that have many weddings now offer premarital instruction in a group format two or three times a year. Anyone who wants to be married in the church must complete the group sessions before their wedding. The sessions are not always led by the minister; some may be led by others with specific expertise in wedding planning.

Financial issues are often the basis for many requests for pastoral care and church assistance. Some churches now require persons who receive financial assistance to complete a financial management seminar. Such churches believe that with proper training in financial management, individuals and families are more likely to avoid financial difficulties in the future. If they refuse the training, they forfeit the right to request further assistance. Many churches have persons qualified to lead these training sessions, and there are a number of excellent resources available to churches for such training.

Ministering to grieving persons can also be done, at least partially, in a group format. Although individual care may also be required, some churches find that grieving people can often minister to one another in a group setting. Several years ago one church had a number of new widows. The pastor was able to bring them together to talk about what was happening in their lives. He found that he had to say little in the meetings because they were able to minister to one another far better than he could. He only had to be a facilitator. The meetings lasted only a few weeks, ending when the women decided they no longer needed to meet.

Providing pastoral care to groups borrows from the twelve-step recovery programs and can be a highly effective way of ministering to people. Leaders of these groups can be specially trained laypersons who can facilitate the meetings. Persons within the groups often minister to one another and hold one another accountable for their progress. Again, this allows the minister and church the opportunity to provide a high level of ministry to these individuals and reduces the amount of time and stress the minister may experience if he or she tried to minister to each person individually.

Counseling

Although this chapter's title included pastoral counseling, the focus has been on pastoral care. Unless the minister is trained in counseling, my advice is to refer all persons who need this help to pastoral counselors or Christian psychologists or psychiatrists. Larger churches may have such a person on staff, but for most small and medium-sized churches trained counselors should be on the minister's pastoral care team and all counseling situations should be quickly referred to them.

Persons who truly need counseling often require much more time than the average minister can give them. Counseling for severe needs may require years of therapy, which few ministers are trained to provide. The danger is that the untrained minister may meet with an individual or couple several times, listen to them, offer advice and prayers, and send them on their way without ever discovering the true issue that created the problem. In such a case, not only is this providing poor ministry, but it also puts the minister and church at risk for a lawsuit. Making a referral is the best way to avoid such problems.

A referral can often identify the people who really don't want a solution to their problems. If they actually had their problems resolved, they wouldn't have anything to talk to people about. In some cases, they have been using their problems to attract sympathy and avoid responsibility for years, and the last thing they want is to have someone ruin that for them. They are more than willing to talk to a minister ad nauseam about their problems, but they are not about to spend money on a counselor who might actually be able to identify their issues and help them resolve them.

A referral puts the burden of resolving a person's problem back on the person and takes it off the minister. If I referred a person to a counselor and he or she refused to go, then I felt I had no further responsibility in the matter. I had made the recommendation I felt would provide the best opportunity for healing, and it was now up to the person to follow it. Moreover I would meet with the person again about the problem only if he or she did begin seeing a counselor, and then only as a pastor checking on his or her progress. This allowed me to remove myself from a role as a counselor, for which I had no training, and permitted me to offer support, prayer, and pastoral care as the person worked through his or her issues. Knowing a person was getting the best care available allowed me to provide the pastoral care he or she needed without the stress I would have experienced if I had been trying to be that person's counselor.

7
Pressures of Relationships

One of the important functions of a church is to provide a place of community. If an individual is unable to experience relationships within the church family, he or she is unlikely to remain in that church for long. However, for many years, ministers have been taught they should not build friendships in their churches. If this is true, where does the minister experience community? What about the minister's family? Should they also avoid establishing relationships with persons in the church? Will some people get jealous if the pastor and family do become close friends with some people in the church? Is this warning about not having friendships in the church valid today, or was it more appropriate for an earlier time? What happens to friendships that do exist when a minister leaves that place of ministry? All of these questions can create a great deal of pressure for the minister and family.

If friendships cannot be enjoyed with church members, could such relationships be developed among peers? That's not always easy either. Some ministers almost view themselves as being in competition with other ministers, so they are unlikely to form strong relationships with those ministers. Sometimes theological differences prevent clergy from developing friendships with other ministers. They don't want to risk being seen as compromising their beliefs. For many it is simply that they don't have time to develop friendships with other ministers. What time they have left from ministry responsibilities they want to spend with their families.

As a result, George Barna has discovered that 61 percent of pastors admit they have few close friends.[1] In a study of clergy wives, 56 percent reported that they felt isolated.[2] This lack of friendships can create problems for the minister and his or her family. We noted in the introduction that ministers now have the second-highest divorce rate among all professionals. Marriage counselors David and Vera Mace noted in 1980 that one of the stresses in clergy marriages was the lack of close relationships with other couples in the church,[3] and this has certainly not improved as we've entered the twenty-first century.

When a minister has no close friendships, he or she has no one to help hold him or her accountable. Such isolation can lead to problems such as addictive behavior, involvement with Internet pornography, and sexual misconduct. Mark Laaser, author of *Healing the Wounds of Sexual Addiction*, notes that three elements in a person's life can lead to sexual addictions: loneliness, anger, and boredom.[4] Some ministers have all three of these elements working in their lives, and when that is coupled with the fact that much of what they do is done in isolation, it is easy to see how ministers can be tempted in this area.

Toxic Friends

There is another area of stress related to the issue of friendships, and that is when the wrong people want to be friends with the pastor. This may cause more stress than the problem of not having any friends. Often these people are controllers in the church, and they want a close relationship with the minister in order to have greater influence. It could be a person who has romantic feelings for the minister and who may resort to behavior ranging from giving the minister gifts to stalking. It could be a person who isn't threatening but whose presence just seems to suck the joy out of the minister's life.

No Friends Outside the Church

Still another stress producer related to friendships can occur when the only friends a minister has are in his or her church. What happens when the minister leaves that church and doesn't have any relationships with people on the outside? What strains will come to a minister's friendships if the church begins to resist the minister's leadership or votes down his or her recommendations? Who will the minister talk to when personal frustration with the church becomes so great that he or she needs the wise and trusted counsel of others?

Karen McClintock identifies another serious issue that can result when a minister has no friendships outside the church he or she is serving. She writes that such a situation can lead ministers to getting their emotional and intimacy needs met within the congregation. . . . The enmeshed congregational system has the same emotional qualities as an incestuous family. When people become too close to one another and the boundaries between individuals are blurred, the stage is set for abuse. These blurred emotional boundaries can lead to the blurring of other boundaries, creating a sense that one can develop any kind of relationship (even a sexual one) within the system, and it will be all right.[5]

Reducing the Pressures of Friendships

Whoever thought it would be so difficult for ministers and their families to have friends or that there would be so many factors to consider? The primary thing to remember is that ministers and their families need close friendships the same as anyone else does, and all of the concerns noted in this chapter can be overcome.

Friends in the Church

Leadership experts James Kouzes and Barry Posner should encourage us when they write, "A managerial myth says we can't get too close to our associates. We can't be friends with people at work. Well, set this myth aside."[6] I agree. No minister can remain at a church for any length of time and not develop friendships with the people. In fact, I wouldn't want to spend much time with people I would not want as friends. Many of the closest friends I have are people whom I served as pastor. At the end of my final service as their pastor I closed by saying, "In a few minutes I will walk out those doors, and I will never again be your pastor, but I will always be your friend." That continues to be our relationship today.

Will some people in the church get jealous because their pastor seems to have a closer friendship with others than he or she does with them? Probably, but how mature is that? Does anyone worry about who their dentist is friends with? I want my dentist to call me by name when she walks into the examination room, but I don't worry about who her friends are when she leaves the office. My insurance agent is a very nice individual, but I have never spent a single minute with him outside of our professional relationship, nor have I lost any sleep over that fact. If people are so insecure and immature that they worry their pastor will develop friendships with people other than them, that is their problem. Why should ministers and their families avoid establishing friendships with people they like in order to not offend the more paranoid members of the church?

The minister has an obligation to serve all people alike. That is one reason I never wanted to know the financial giving of anyone in our church. I did not want that information to ever influence me in the way I relate to people. I tried to meet people's needs as best I could without showing any favoritism. However, that does not mean my wife and I went out to dinner with everyone in the church. It certainly did not mean I shared my more personal thoughts and concerns with every congregation member.

A minister should expect to enjoy different levels of friendships with people in the church. There were individuals I spent hours with fishing. There were some I played golf with, and still do today. There were a few my wife and I enjoyed spending time with trying out new restaurants and browsing around in bookstores. There were only a very few that we could share our hearts with and not fear them judging us or violating our confidence in them.

For ministers, having friends in the churches they serve does require some guidelines. Ministers must keep confidences and must not violate those confidences, even when talking to close friends. There are just some things that cannot be discussed with anyone. Even if it sometimes means being misunderstood, those confidences must be kept, and good friends will understand that.

Keeping church issues separate from the friendship is also important. There have been times when friends in our church disagreed with me over some action I was asking the church to take. We had to learn to agree to disagree and keep our friendships at a different level than our pastor/parishioner roles. Sometimes these disagreements may have strained friendships, but the friendships always outlasted the disagreements.

Friendships with Peers

Some ministers find it easier to make friendships with ministers from other denominations than they do with those from the denomination they serve. Perhaps they see these persons as less of a threat, or maybe they just enjoy widening their circle of friendships in order to get a different perspective on ministry.

Ministers sometimes need other people they can talk to about issues with which they may be struggling, and people from different denominations may seem safe to talk to. They bring different perspectives from different polities, and their judicatories may have different approaches to an issue. That can provide ministers with new and helpful insights.

Regardless of whether ministers seek friendships with ministers from their own denominations or from other denominations, they need friends who are in the ministry. No one can better understand the issues a minister faces than another minister. No one can better empathize with the doubts and fears that ministers sometimes have than another minister. Ministers need relationships with their colleagues for encouragement and support.

Is there a risk in developing friendships with other ministers? Yes, but there is always a danger in making friends. Friends can be disappointing. They can be harmful. They can be disloyal. But most won't do any of those things. A greater risk is in not having friendships with other ministers, because that will make a minister feel as if he or she is in this alone, and that Lone Ranger syndrome is never healthy.

Can a minister be friends with his or her judicatory leader? Some ministers are concerned that such a relationship would be awkward and that relationships with judicatory leaders should be kept purely professional. Friendships can be strained if a conflict arises in the church the pastor serves requiring the intervention of the judicatory leader, who then finds the pastor was partly responsible for the conflict. As a judicatory leader I have had to suggest to a couple of pastors that they should consider resigning their churches because they had become lightning rods for conflict. My suggestion did not impact the relationships I had with the ministers, but it could have if we had been close friends.

Most of the relationships I have with the pastors I serve are good and healthy, but they are primarily professional. The few exceptions are ministers with whom I had closer relationships when I was a pastor.

Friendships with Persons Outside the Church

Healthy ministers will want to develop friendships with people outside their own congregation and denominational circles. Many of these friendships should be with persons who are not currently Christians. Too many ministers live in a church bubble that prevents them from having contact with nonbelievers. As a bivocational pastor I worked in a factory forty hours a week. I knew exactly what life in the working world was like and what members of my congregation faced every day at work. Some ministers do not have that experience, and they never will unless they develop friendships with persons outside the church.

Making friends with nonbelievers will sometimes lead to misunderstandings, especially by good church people who cannot understand why their minister wants to associate with "people like that." One of the problems in many churches is that few people do have friendships with people who are not already part of the church. Jesus taught us that we are to be a light in dark places that will attract people to him, and we can't do that if we are not willing to spend time with people who are not Christians. Neil Cole reminds us that "if you want to win this world to Christ, you are going to have to sit in the smoking section. That is where lost people are found, and if you make them put their cigarette out to hear the message, they will be thinking about only one thing: 'When can I get another cigarette?'"[7]

I am not advocating that ministers make friends with non-Christians just so they can witness to them. Hopefully, a minister's faith is so contagious and he or she is so passionate about his or her relationship with Jesus Christ that a minister's non-Christian friends would be drawn to Christ, but that is not why ministers should have friendships with non-Christians. Ministers should make friends with non-Christians because some of them are really neat and enjoyable people to be with. Every year I attend a blues concert and spend the weekend with the same group of people. Some are Christians; some are not. Some drink a beer while I drink a soft drink. Some smoke a cigarette while I do not. We all eat way too much barbequed food, laugh, and have a great time listening to some really good music. That may offend some church folks, but I believe that is exactly the kind of place where Jesus would be. In fact, on more than one occasion the religious crowd criticized him because he was willing to associate with known sinners (see Matt. 9:9-13; Luke 19:1-10).

Non-Christian friendships also provide the minister with a different perspective on life. If ministers spend the majority of their time preparing biblical sermons, reading Christian books, meeting with other Christians, and listening to Christian radio stations, they should not be surprised to find the world is changing rapidly and leaving them behind.

As a child I was raised on a dairy farm. Dairy cows have to be milked twice a day, and between milking is when the crops have to be planted and harvested, the hay baled and brought to the barn, and all the other necessary farm chores performed. Needless to say, we didn't get away from the farm much.

In the milking parlor we kept a radio tuned to a country music station. That was the only radio station I ever listened to. In the sixth or seventh grade our class was asked to pick their top rock-and-roll singers. As I looked at the list of performers, I didn't recognize a single name. My classmates could not believe I had never heard of Elvis Presley and the other well-known rock-and-roll singers of the late 1950s. I still remember being embarrassed, but I was never exposed to that style of music or the rock-and-roll phenomenon.

Ministers who have only Christian friends and live within a Christian vacuum will discover someday that they have nothing to say about the issues that matter to other people. They won't even know what those issues are. They will still be answering questions that people stopped asking years earlier.

Making Friends

Although ministers are in a place of leadership and are often upfront before the people, many of them are extremely introverted. Making friends is not easy for them. Many prefer the safety of their studies and books. How can such persons make friends with others? The simplest answer is for them to be friends to the people with whom they want to establish relationships.

A person should begin looking for people who share his or her interests. If he or she enjoys playing golf or fishing, finding others who enjoy the same activities shouldn't be difficult. If a person enjoys browsing through bookstores, he or she will likely see in those bookstores some of the same people time and again who also enjoy spending time in bookstores. A friendship can begin with something as simple as a smile and an introduction. A few minutes of conversation is all that is needed for people to decide if they have common tastes in golf, fishing, or books and if a relationship is possible. At this point the goal is not to find a "best friend" with whom to share one's deepest thoughts. The goal is just to find a friend.

Perhaps a minister's family goes to the same place each year on vacation. Our daughter and her family go to the same beach approximately the same time each year. They always stay in the same motel, and the owners now call them by name when they walk into the lobby to register. The owners even remember the children's names. Many of the other people in the motel are also there year after year, and our daughter and her family have made acquaintances with many of these people. They have also made friends with another family, and they look forward to spending that week of vacation with them. These people were once strangers to our daughter's family. At first they had few things in common: each family enjoyed spending vacation on the same beach, staying in the same motel each year, and each had young children about the same age. The two families became friends because they were friendly toward one another. They began conversing and discovered they shared other common interests.

Very seldom does anyone find a friend. A person must make friends, and he or she begins that process by being friendly toward others. Identifying other people who might have some things in common and then reaching out to them is an effective way to begin creating a relationship. It's all right to test the waters and see if a relationship will go beyond a casual acquaintance and develop into a friendship. If a relationship doesn't seem to go anywhere, a person should not worry about it. He or she just needs to continue looking. Eventually that person will begin to develop friendships with different people that will enrich his or her life and be a blessing to his or her family.

8

Pressures of Being Alone

This chapter is a natural follow-up to the preceding chapter. Regardless of whether a minister has few friends or many, there are times when he or she is very alone. People tell the minister details about their lives that cannot be shared with another human being. Even if the minister sees the other person being misunderstood by others, he or she must not break the confidences that have been made. One minister heard members of his church question the actions of a church family. He knew the personal pain that led that family to make the decisions they made, but he could not share that information with others. He did the only thing he could do; he continued to encourage the family and pray for them—alone.

Ministers often must make decisions that will not be understood by everyone in the church, and yet if he or she is to be a leader in the congregation, such decisions must be made regardless of their popularity. J. Oswald Sanders reminds us that leaders must always be ahead of their followers.[1] One cannot lead from the middle of the pack or from the back. Like Moses in the wilderness, the minister must be out front seeking to lead congregation members in the direction God lays out for them. And like Moses, the minister should expect to be criticized and questioned. His or her integrity will sometimes even be questioned. In the face of such criticism the minister can often do nothing except continue to seek God's direction—alone.

Much of ministry occurs when the minister is alone. He or she has sermons to prepare, and long hours are often spent each week in the study. The minister not only has to study the Scriptures to prepare the message each week but also ensure he or she is personally prepared to deliver it. While others can give most of their attention to the present age, the minister will experience "an isolation of the soul that feels the responsibility of eternal issues and must maintain its commitment to divine purposes above all else"[2] if he or she wishes to speak an eternal word to the congregation.

Such loneliness can have devastating effects on the minister, his or her family, and the church. Christian psychologist Archibald Hart tells us that "it is a psychological fact that one cannot resolve conflict and clarify issues simply by thinking about them."[3] Ministers need others with whom they can discuss these issues, or they risk making poor decisions that benefit no one.

Depression can result when a minister feels all alone in his or her work. If a person believes there is no one he or she can talk to, that person can experience such intense stress that his or her body chemistry can change and cause depression. This type of depression, known as endogenous depression, is experienced by many ministers[4] and is sometimes difficult to understand and treat because it may not occur until long after the stressors have been removed.

In one study, feeling isolated and lonely was one of the top four reasons clergy identified for their leaving the ministry.[5] Ministers who believe they have no one they can confide in are more likely to experience burnout. Interestingly enough, these same ministers are usually the Lone Ranger types who do not involve themselves in the wider denominational body nor even in a local ministerial group. Part of their isolation is their own choice, but they find that it can soon lead to a very lonely ministry.

Isolation and loneliness can cause an even greater problem; it can lead to sexual addictions and misconduct. We saw in the previous chapter on friendships that ministers operate in an environment that makes them susceptible to sexual addictions such as pornography, and this environment includes the feeling of being isolated. Dean Hoge and Jacqueline Wenger found that 75 percent of the people who left the ministry due to sexual misconduct indicated that they were lonely and felt isolated from others.[6] Even more disturbing is that approximately 30 percent of ministers have anonymously reported they have been sexually intimate with someone in their parish.[7]

There is no question that the stress of feeling isolated in the ministry can have devastating effects on the minister, his or her family, and the church. Yet there are many aspects of ministry that cannot be easily shared. How can this stress be reduced and the minister no longer feel so alone as he or she fulfills the calling God has on his or her life?

Reducing the Pressures Related to Being Alone

Ministers may not always be free to share everything with other people, but that does not mean they need to be alone. No matter what size of ministry is being served, ministers need to create ministry teams to help them carry the burden of leadership. In larger churches that may include the ministerial staff, while laypersons will need to be on the team in smaller churches. These teams provide the minister someone to assist with decision making and conflict resolution. The teams should be made up of spiritual persons of the highest integrity who know the value of keeping confidences. This allows the minister to share things with them that might have to otherwise be kept private. Such teams also provide the minister with trusted allies to whom he can share his or her own challenges and frustrations.

Team members do not have to be included on the list of the minister's friends, but they do have to share the same vision for the ministry as the minister. It is fine if they don't always agree with the minister. In fact, having people who are not afraid to challenge the minister's thinking is a healthy thing because that often leads to better decisions.

In addition to being godly people, team members should be competent. If I was putting together a team, I would want people of proven leadership abilities. Too often, especially in smaller churches, people are selected for leadership positions because of their family name or their length of time in the church and not for their leadership gifts. Having worked in smaller churches throughout my ministry I am aware of the land mines that exist if these people are not selected, but I am also aware of the difficulties created otherwise. A leadership team is only as strong as its weakest link, and having a spiritually immature, negative, and visionless controller on the leadership team will only weaken it and reduce its effectiveness.

A strong leadership team will help reduce the sense of isolation that many ministers feel and will strengthen the overall effectiveness of the ministry. Such a team will also challenge the minister and help keep him or her accountable by reducing the possibility of the minister making poor moral choices.

Prayer Team

Along with a leadership team, ministers must develop a prayer team to come alongside and pray for the minister, the minister's family, and the church. John Maxwell contributes his success at Skyline Wesleyan Church in San Diego to the creation of a prayer team. It started with a man by the name of Bill Klassen who wanted to pray for Maxwell. Klassen began to organize a group who would pray for their pastor and the church services. That prayer group grew from thirty-one people to one hundred and twenty and had an enormous impact on Maxwell and the church.[8] Maxwell regularly encourages ministers to develop prayer partners in their own ministries.

In 1997 three men from our church and I attended the Promise Keeper's event in Washington DC. On the trip home they asked if they could meet with me once a week for prayer. They felt God leading them to begin a special time of prayer for me and my family. Every Sunday evening for the next three years a group of us met for a half hour of prayer. The number of people never grew beyond eight, but that time of prayer led to some amazing ministry in our small church. It also did some wonderful things for me because I knew that no matter how challenging a week I may have, on Sunday evening a group of people who loved and believed in me would surround me with their prayers. I also knew they were praying for me throughout the week as well. If I ever returned to pastoral ministry, one of the first things I would establish in the church would be a minister's prayer team that would meet with me weekly to pray for the church, my family, and me.

Trusted Colleagues

It is not healthy for a minister to carry everyone's secrets alone. Ministers need persons with whom they can share some of the burdens they carry for other people. That may be another minister in another community or a judicatory leader. It could be a trained counselor the minister sees on a regular basis or as needed. A counselor would be especially needed if the minister is seeking professional advice on how to help an individual address a specific issue.

The key is to not violate confidentiality. This can be done by talking about the issue and not the individual and talking to persons who would not know the individual. In no case should the individual be named or identified in any way.

As a judicatory leader pastors will sometimes call me when they have been wounded by persons within their churches. They are able to share with me their pain and frustration over the actions of these persons without identifying them. In very few cases has a pastor ever named the person(s) responsible for the pain. In the chapter on friendship I indicated that judicatory ministers may not be the best persons for a friendship, but they are usually good persons with whom ministers can share some of their deepest burdens.

Being part of a ministerial group can help a minister avoid the sense of being alone. Such groups may meet once a month, often for breakfast or lunch. Some have set agendas for their meetings, while others keep them unstructured. A group setting is not the place for a minister to begin unloading all his or her issues, but it is a good way to build relationships with other local ministers and learn their ministerial challenges. A minister may even find a colleague with whom he or she can establish a deeper relationship and gain wise counsel and direction.

Coaches

Many executives in the business world now receive life and professional coaches as one of the perks of their positions. Their organizations believe that having a coach will benefit the executive and thus benefit the organization as well. Some of these executive coaches can be quite expensive, so these organizations are investing much in their hope that this practice will return a dividend to the company.

As usual, churches lag well behind the business community when it comes to acknowledging the value of coaching, but some ministers are now seeing its benefits. For the past couple of years I have had the opportunity of coaching several ministers who have all agreed that it has been a helpful experience. In most cases, these ministers lived several states away. I did not know them except for what they shared with me on the telephone, so I was a safe person for them to discuss whatever issues they might have. I, in turn, could ask them questions that helped them make necessary decisions without directly telling them what to do.

When I began coaching ministers, I was not ready for the deep emotions that often came out. As I indicated, most of these ministers were strangers to me. Our relationship was purely professional. Yet more than a few of them at times broke out in tears as they shared information with me that they had kept bottled up for months or years.

I often heard them say, "This is the first time I've been able to tell anyone about this." Their pain was deep, and their relief was obvious as they were able to share secrets they had not felt free to tell anyone else.

In my opinion, every minister needs a coach to whom he or she can confide and seek direction. The coach does not need to be someone who has been in the ministry, though such a coach would understand the unique challenges the minister faces. The coaching relationship is simple to establish. The main challenge is finding the right person to serve as a coach, and a minister may need to interview several coaches before finding the right person.

Spiritual Directors

Another important person who can help the minister feel less alone is a spiritual director. It seems odd that those of us in ministry who are often called upon to act as spiritual directors for those we serve so seldom have spiritual directors ourselves. Eugene Peterson observes that this was not always so. He comments that at one time ministers were assumed to have spiritual directors as part of their job descriptions.[9] Peterson writes that "spiritual direction takes place when two people agree to give their full attention to what God is doing in one (or both) of their lives and seek to respond in faith."[10] Spiritual direction requires time and intentionality from each person for it to be effective. It is work that often goes unseen by others but is essential for the spiritual well-being and growth of the minister.

Perhaps one reason so few ministers today have a spiritual director is that they often prefer to do things on their own. They don't want others holding them accountable for their spiritual development. They perhaps reason that a spiritual director may be all right for those who are spiritually immature, but not for someone in the ministry. Such an attitude is little more than a cover for pride and should in itself convince ministers even more strongly that they do need a spiritual director.

Much of the isolation ministers feel comes out of the things they do that many people consider to be ministry. Spiritual direction focuses on the development of the inner person. As ministers open their inner beings up to becoming more of what God would have them to be, they find ministry to be less of a struggle. They are developing the inner resources to handle almost anything ministry can throw at them. It is when they neglect the inner development of their souls that they find they lack the spiritual resources to cope with the challenges of ministry. Spiritual directors are vital because they help keep ministers focused on that inner development.

Finding a spiritual director may be difficult and take longer than one would like. A spiritual director must believe in the one seeking direction and yet not be hesitant to challenge that individual and hold him or her accountable. A spiritual director should be someone who can understand a person's spiritual needs and can guide him or her in that area. A spiritual director should also be someone with whom a person is comfortable and whose company he or she enjoys. Spiritual direction means meeting at least once a month and talking about the deeper issues of one's life, so a person must find someone he or she likes and can trust completely.

The search for a spiritual director should begin with a prayer for God's help in finding the right person. It is important not to hurry and select someone that later proves to be a poor choice. Selecting a spiritual director means a person should spend time thinking about everyone in his or her life and praying about each one. God may even bring someone new into the picture. By being sensitive to the Spirit's leading, a person will eventually find someone who is just right and can then ask that individual to be his or her spiritual director.

God

We are never alone. No matter how alone we may feel, God has promised to never leave nor forsake his children (see Heb. 13:5). One of the values of a spiritual director is that he or she can help remind a minister of this wonderful truth when he or she feels so alone in ministry. It's not that ministers don't know that God has promised to be with them; it's just that it is easy for them to forget it when they feel isolated.

I identify best with the biblical characters that didn't always have it together. Elijah is one of my favorites because I can see so much of myself in him. In 1 Kings 18 Elijah has a great victory over the false prophets of Baal on Mount Carmel. In the very next chapter he hears that Queen Jezebel has promised to take his life, so he flees to Mount Horeb. When God meets him there, Elijah tells the Lord that he is the only one left who is faithful to God.

The reason I identify with Elijah is that most of my greatest struggles in ministry have come shortly after a spiritual victory. Something or someone causes my victory to be short lived. In such times it is easy for me to get discouraged and feel that I am all alone in the ministry. I become convinced that not only does no one understand what I'm feeling but no one even cares. More than once I've looked at my wife and said, "Honey, we're all alone in this." Of course, we weren't, and she has always been faithful to remind me of that. Just as God reminded Elijah that there were seven thousand in Israel who had never bowed the knee to Baal, she has often reminded me that we are surrounded by many people who believe in us and trust our leadership and our ministry to them. Even more importantly, she reminds me, God has certainly not abandoned us.

When ministers feel the burden of ministry is becoming greater than they can handle and they are feeling isolated from others, they need to deepen their relationship with God. They can do this by not neglecting their personal time with him and by spending time in prayer and in the Scriptures. They should also think back to the time God called them into the ministry and the joy and excitement they felt when they responded. Ministers then need to sit back and allow God to minister to them. They need to let themselves rest in his arms and allow him to replace the heavy yoke of ministry with the lighter yoke he promised to his children. Do I sound like someone who is talking from experience? Believe me, I am, and I've never had God disappoint me.

9
Pressures of Conflict

Conflict is inevitable in ministry regardless of the size of the church, its denominational polity, its theology, or the expertise of the church staff and lay leaders. Churches are made up of people, and whenever people are involved, there is the potential for conflict. It is certain that conflict will arise in every ministry, but what is uncertain is when it will occur and what it will be about.

I recently read a story about a young minister's experience in his first church after seminary. He had only been there a few weeks when the church matriarch marched into his office and told him, "There isn't room in this church for me and you, and I'm not leaving. Either change your sermons or pack your suitcases." He learned later that she wasn't kidding and that she had had that conversation with other pastors before him. As the reader might imagine, the pastor did not last long at that church.

Fortunately, I've never had a *High Noon* showdown like that, but like all ministers I've had my share of conflicts from being in the ministry. I am a classic conflict avoider, so conflict of any magnitude creates great amounts of stress for me. Like most ministers I want people to like me, and I tend to see conflict as a personal attack on me as a person and a minister. I know that isn't usually the case, but I'm hardwired to see conflict that way.

Clearly this isn't healthy for the minister or the ministry he or she serves. It can prevent the minister from making decisions that will positively impact his or her ministry. The only way to avoid conflict is to do nothing, and too many ministers and churches are doing exactly that because of previous conflicts that have caused great harm to the church.

Churches that have experienced conflicts are likely to avoid any change that might upset the peace that currently exists. Tom Bandy declares that "the Christian church has become just another cult in the pagan world. . . . It is the cult of harmony."[1] We prefer harmony over truth or mission. We will do anything to avoid conflict even if that means giving veto power to a handful of controllers who are more committed to maintaining the status quo than to mission. For proof we only have to look at the worship wars that exist in many churches today and the refusal of many churches to reach out to anyone who isn't just like the current membership.

The sad thing about this is that this occurs in many churches that have a majority of people who want to see change occur and want to see new people reached for the gospel. Bandy points out that about 20 percent of a church's membership may be made up of controllers but another 60 percent of the membership is committed to peace and unity. Members in this last group are unwilling to do anything that might cause the church to lose people if changes are implemented.[2] This means that church leaders can expect that up to 80 percent of their members will automatically be against any change the first time they hear it and that any proposed change is likely to result in conflict. If ministers are unwilling to engage conflict, they will be unable to lead their ministries in any significant growth, and their ministries will suffer.

Avoiding conflict also has an impact on the personal life of the minister. His or her family will experience the effects of the conflict either from what they hear at the church or from what the minister says and does at home. It can affect the minister's relationship with his or her family, and he or she may have less energy to give to the family because he or she feels so drained by the conflict.

The minister's sleeping and eating may be affected. He or she may begin to doubt his or her abilities or call to the ministry. Stress can build up and cause additional physical, emotional, and spiritual problems. Intense stress can cause the minister to have panic attacks or experience waves of cascading fear.

Nothing good comes from unresolved conflict. Since conflict is unavoidable in a growing ministry, the healthiest thing a minister can do is to learn how to handle conflict and make it his or her friend rather than a mortal enemy.

Reducing the Stress of Conflict

The first thing a minister must do is to stop thinking of conflict as a bad thing. Certainly, it can become a negative in the church, but it can also be a positive. A ministry cannot make any major, and sometimes minor, changes without conflict.[3] When changes are proposed in a church, the first thought many people will have is, *How will this affect me and my role in the church?* As mentioned earlier, controllers see most change as a threat to their role and will seek to block change to preserve their own sense of self-worth. They won't come out and say that is what they are doing. Instead, they will dress their actions up in more spiritual clothing, but if they are pushed hard enough, their true motives will soon surface.

The leader's task is to frame the issues in a way that the people can see the opportunities and challenges the issues present to the ministry.[4] People are unwilling to change until they believe the benefits of the change are greater than the cost. Focusing only on the changes almost guarantees that the opposition will increase, especially from those who prefer harmony at any price. This opposition only heightens the conflict until the proposed changes are finally dropped. Helping people see the benefits rather than just looking at the changes needed to produce the benefits gives the people something else to discuss. If they can see desired benefits resulting from the changes, their opposition will decrease and so will the potential for conflict.

A classic example of this can be found in Martin Luther King Jr.'s famous "I Have a Dream" speech in 1963. He knew racial reconciliation would be difficult to achieve. It would require enormous changes in the way many people thought and related to one another. Some would never be able to make the changes, and they still haven't even today. The impact of this speech can never be overstated. It took the focus away from the changes, which many would resist, to a future that few people could deny would be preferable to the hatred and violence that existed between the races. As people began to grasp the benefits the nation would enjoy when the racial walls that divided this nation came down, many of them welcomed the changes that would bring the races together.

The minister not only needs to refocus the congregation on the benefits of the change but also needs to understand how to control the temperature of the conflict. At times turning the heat up will be necessary, but there are also times when the heat needs to be turned down so that the congregation is not paralyzed by the conflict.[5] This is as much an art as it is a science, and it requires the minister knows the congregation and is able to regularly take its temperature. Failing to do so makes it more unlikely that the changes will be implemented and more likely that the conflict will escalate.

Bring Conflict Out into the Open

Conflict is most damaging when it remains hidden. If we believe that conflict is normal in any system that includes human beings, then we need to bring it out into the open when it occurs.[6] Conflict cannot be addressed when it is hidden. There are few things more damaging to a church than for the minister to hear that "some people" are unhappy, but these "people" are never identified. These anonymous people can do a ministry a great deal of harm while making it difficult for anyone to respond to their concerns.

A pastor friend of mine had been very frustrated at her current place of ministry for much of the past year. Rumors had been circulating about problems in the church, but she was unable to identify the source of the rumors or the reason for them. Several people left the church. They assured her that she was not the reason they were leaving, but they wouldn't tell her why they were leaving. One Sunday after the service she confronted congregation members and asked them to please tell her the problems they believed existed in the church. No one spoke, although it was obvious that problems did exist. She finally resigned from that church because of the impact it was having on her and her family.

Another church saw nearly a third of the congregation leave within a period of about a year. In that situation, much of the turmoil was centered on the pastor and his wife. Even though the focus of this conflict was well-known, the leadership refused to address it in a meaningful way. I encouraged them to bring together the dissatisfied people and the pastor and his wife and discuss the issues that were dividing the church. They refused to be proactive until their congregation dwindled down to two-thirds of its former size at which time the minister resigned. The church is now slowly trying to rebuild, but it lost many good people in the process.

When the conflict is in the open and people can discuss it like adults, there is a much greater chance of resolving it. A problem occurs if the church has an unspoken rule that says Christians don't fight. A ministry operating with that rule will often be a place with a number of conflicts going on because no one is willing to confront either the conflicts or the rule that keeps such conflicts hidden in the shadows of church life.

One way of bringing a conflict into the open is to allow other people to know about it. At first, this may sound self-defeating because the more people who know there is a conflict, the greater likelihood that other conflicts will break out. No one likes to air their dirty laundry. However, Speed Leas believes that "encouraging the others to join with you in dealing with the conflict and encouraging the others to stay with you in the process is perhaps the single most important conflict management skill one can use."[7]

As a judicatory minister I have worked with some churches whose pastors were forced to resign by the leadership boards. In some instances many in the congregation did not know of any differences between the pastor and board. When the board's actions became public knowledge, these persons were understandably upset. They felt they had been left out of the discussion and that the board had acted without congregational input. In my denomination the calling and terminating of ministers is usually the responsibility of the entire congregation and not the board, but in practice many church boards have forced ministers to resign. The usual excuse is to protect the church from the turmoil and pain of voting on keeping the minister or letting him or her go.

However, there is often much greater pain and turmoil when congregation members learn they have been left out of the discussion about their minister. More than once I've had church members tell me they would never let the board do that to the church again. Hostility sometimes is created between the board and members of the congregation who feel betrayed and powerless. This hostility often results in divisions and distrust between factions in the church that negatively impacts the ministry of the church for years. It might help to remember that people who feel powerless and believe their voice will not be heard are the ones who are most likely to fight dirty. People who are invited to be part of the conversation are more likely to work toward the resolution of a conflict in a way that benefits everyone rather than seeking to win at all costs.

Unite Around the Vision

Conflict is often nothing more than two visions competing for the same space. Any time I have been involved in a conflict consultation with a church, I have asked different ones to tell me the vision of the church. No one in the conflicted church was able to do so, which is one reason for the conflict. I recently asked that same question of committee members in a conflicted church. They assured me the church had a vision statement, but no one could tell me what it was. The committee chair started to look it up in his notebook until I told him that if he had to look it up, it didn't count. For a vision to have any meaning to a church it must be more than a written statement that is framed, posted in the church office, and never looked at again. It must be the driving force behind everything the church does, and it must be known by everyone in the church.

Uniting the congregation around a commonly accepted vision of a preferred future for the church is thus an important way to avoid conflict. This makes it less likely that some in the church will have one vision while another group has a completely different vision. It gives the church added focus and helps keep everyone working together toward the same goal. New ministries become easier to start because anything that fits the vision is automatically approved. Anything that would distract the church from fulfilling its God-given vision is automatically rejected even if it seems like a good idea.

There are many excellent resources to help a church identify the vision God has for them, so we won't go into detail about how to do that here. It will suffice to say that the vision must fit the core values and bedrock beliefs of the church and align with the spiritual gifts of the congregation, the passions of the people, and the needs of the community. God will not give a church a vision that does not match all these elements.

Not only will having a common vision for the church reduce the number of conflicts, but it will also serve as a point of reference to stop conflicts when they do occur. The question is simply "Is what we are doing, or proposing to do, in agreement with the vision of the church?" If the answer is yes, the conflict should be lessened if not eliminated.

Addressing Conflict Centered on Personalities

So far we have looked at conflict associated with changes being proposed or implemented in the church. This tends to be a simpler type of conflict to address. The more difficult conflict to resolve is personality driven. Sometimes two or more people in a church simply do not like each other. It is sad that this can be true of Christians, but though the Holy Spirit is available to help his people truly love one another, they do not always keep in step with him and they let personality differences get in their way. As we all know, this can lead to conflict within the church.

Many ministers find personality-driven conflict the most stressful. Such conflict often puts a minister in the middle of the turmoil either because the minister is a party involved in the conflict or because the conflicting parties are trying to draw the minister to their side of the battle.

When a minister finds that he or she is the lightning rod of conflict with another person or group within the church, he or she needs to confront the conflict as quickly as possible. Conflict avoiders want to believe that if they ignore the problem, it will go away. It won't; usually it only gets worse. As soon as the minister learns that someone is upset with him or her, the minister must begin dialogue with that individual or group as soon as possible. Matthew 5:23-24 teaches that Christians are to go to anyone who has something against them and seek reconciliation. As the leader it is the minister's responsibility to go to the other person to try to resolve the conflict.

At one of his conferences I once heard John Maxwell tell about a time he was watching railroad cars being added to a train. He noticed that the engine always moved toward the cars. The cars never moved toward the engine. A principle he learned from that is that leaders must make the first move toward those who follow them. I think this would certainly apply when someone has an issue with the minister that is creating conflict.

Although it is never easy to do, the minister must determine the truths behind the other person's unhappiness. John Paul Lederach calls this prayerful vulnerability.[8] When we approach someone who is upset with us, we should not do so with the intention of defending ourselves but with an attitude of listening and prayerfully discerning what is true about that person's claims against us. This can be a time not only of reconciliation but also of growth as we may begin to see some things about ourselves that we had never seen before. We should not apologize for things that are not true, but we should certainly be willing to apologize for the things that are true and use this time as an opportunity to change and grow as individuals.

Clearly, there are some people with whom we can never be reconciled. John Maxwell has a principle of getting along with people that he calls the Bob principle. He writes, "If Bob has problems with Bill, and Bob has problems with Fred, and Bob has problems with Sue, and Bob has problems with Jane, and Bob has problems with Sam, then Bob is usually the problem."[9] We are unlikely to ever reconcile with the Bobs (or Bobbies) in the world because they don't want reconciliation. Their identity is found in their ability to identify perceived problems or transmit the concerns of others to everyone they can. The Bobs and Bobbies in the church need to be confronted with the damage they are doing to the organization, and their influence must be negated as much as possible.

The other personality-driven conflict that creates pressure for the minister doesn't directly involve him or her but involves others within the ministry who want the minister to join their side in the battle. In conflict management this is known as triangulation. At this point a minister must be very careful about anything he or she says because people will start using the minister's words to reinforce their position: "The pastor said . . ." or "The pastor agrees that . . ." In my current role things I have said casually to a member of one of the churches I serve have been used to promote a position I may or may not agree with.

Recently, I met with the pastor and board of a church to discuss some problems the church was having, including some of its financial difficulties. I told them their financial problem was becoming increasingly common for churches their size. They expressed a concern about being able to keep their fully funded pastor, who had served them for several years. I encouraged them to consider conducting stewardship teaching in the church because the giving level in their church was low. I also challenged them to identify ways they could reach out into the community more effectively. I told them that some churches of their size were moving toward having bivocational ministers instead of fully funded pastors because of economics and that if they didn't find ways to increase attendance and giving, they might have to do the same thing. All the board heard was that "churches of their size were moving toward having bivocational ministers." As the board members prepared the budget for the New Year, they told their pastor his salary would have to be reduced. After all his years of faithful service, he had to seek a new place of employment to support his family. The board members justified their actions by referencing my words about "churches their size" becoming bivocational.

Ministers who refuse to take sides in a personality-driven conflict will often find themselves declared the enemy by both sides and may find both sides turning against them. While it is essential that sides not be taken, the conflict cannot be ignored either. A minister can offer to act as a mediator between the two sides, bringing them both to the table to begin discussing the problems dividing them. This allows the minister the opportunity to bring healing to the matter without further disruption.

It is probably best that the minister not be the sole mediator in such a dispute. A lay leader in the church who is known to be godly and who both sides trust should assist the minister in the mediation process. This will help keep the minister from overlooking important issues in the conflict and halt further attempts at triangulation by either party. Having an additional mediator also provides another voice when recommendations about how to resolve the issue are needed. If one party is found primarily at fault in the matter, that party will be less likely to blame the minister for being biased if another person has shared in the mediation. Finally, mediation between two warring groups within a church is always a stressful time, and having someone as a prayer partner and a companion through the process will help reduce some of that tension.

Outside Assistance

Most churches wait too long to bring in outside assistance. By the time conflict consultants are brought in to help resolve an issue, there has usually already been irreparable damage done to the church family. People have left the church, finances are down, guests sense the tension that exists and don't return, and the minister's ability to lead the church is often compromised. In fact, conflict management consultant Ed Peirce believes that half of the ministers harmed by a phase three conflict (see below) leave the ministry never to return.[10] That is a huge loss the kingdom of God cannot afford.

Phase one conflicts are those minor dustups that occur from time to time in every organization. The minister can often lead the church to resolve those conflicts. However, if the conflict escalates to a phase two conflict, the minister is unlikely to be able to lead the church to resolve it.[11]

In a phase two conflict people are beginning to feel hurt and seek out others who feel as they do. Lines within the church are being drawn and an "us" versus "them" mentality is formed. It's not a Hatfield-Mc-Coy feud yet, but it may become one if the issue isn't resolved soon. Communication is reduced because neither side wants to give out information that might give the other side an advantage. Everything is given a spiritual meaning, and people claim they are only concerned with the well-being of the church.[12] When the conflict enters this stage, the church should bring in outside consultants to help resolve the conflict before it can go to the next level.

A phase three conflict develops when the loosely formed gatherings of a phase two conflict consolidate into identifiable groups. Leaders emerge within these groups, who begin to recruit others to join their sides. Issues are no longer the center of the conflict; people are. In a phase three conflict, resolving the original problem is less important than winning the battle. In the first two phases of conflict a win-win for both parties is possible, but in a phase three conflict someone will usually have to lose to satisfy the other party. Outside consultants will almost always have to be brought in for there to be any hope of resolution. Pastors are seldom able to lead the church in resolving a phase three conflict and in many cases will have to leave the church even if they were not responsible for the initial conflict. As noted earlier, many of these pastors will leave the ministry completely.

Some judicatories have trained conflict management teams to respond to their churches that are going through conflict. In our judicatory we have invested much money and time in training a number of ministers and laypersons to serve on conflict management teams. When a church contacts the director of this ministry, the director begins gathering a team of people who have no geographic or other ties to the church. The team members meet with the church and follow a process they learned in their training. They meet with individuals and groups to determine the roots of the problem and later bring specific recommendations to the church for ways to resolve the conflict. The pastor of the conflicted church is never a part of the team but is interviewed just as others in the church are interviewed. Because of the polity of church autonomy in my denomination, the church is free to accept the recommendations and implement them or reject them. Those who do attempt to implement the recommendations often experience healing and, in time, are able to move forward in ministry. The cost to the churches for this service is minimal.

Independent churches and churches in judicatories that do not have this ministry available to them can find a number of conflict consultants who work with churches. Their cost will usually be substantially higher, but it still pales in comparison to the cost to the church for doing nothing. It is important to find a consultant who understands the church and the specific polity of the particular church or denomination. Whether a church uses an independent consultant or a judicatory conflict management team, the key to success is to call them in before the conflict escalates to the point that there is little left to be salvaged.

Unhealthy Systems

Although conflict is normal in churches, there is a problem when the same conflict is repeated again and again without being resolved.[13] Some churches lose their pastors every two or three years because they pressure the ministers to leave. Some churches are able to grow to a certain size before a blowup causes a number of the new people to leave and reduce the church back to a more comfortable (for some) size. Individuals or families in churches renew their unresolved animosity toward one another on a regular basis and create problems within the church. Whenever conflicts resurface, the church is dealing with more than just a conflict; it is dealing with an unhealthy system. Resolving the conflict is impossible until the system creating it is addressed.

Because this is the only system the longtime members of the church know, they will have difficultly realizing something is wrong. Before I entered the ministry, the church our family attended was caught up in yet another conflict. A lay leader confided in me that he didn't understand why every time the church seemed ready to move into a new level of ministry, something like this always happened. My first thought was that I was talking to one of the reasons. He and his wife were behind many of the conflicts the church had, but no one in the church would confront them or others who seemed responsible. We had a system that permitted disruptive people to have positions of power in the church, and they used their power to control almost everything in the church.

A minister is usually unable to help the church address systemic issues. They existed long before he or she came to the church, and they appear normal to the members. An outside consultant is needed to help identify the root causes of the ongoing problems. The recommendations for change will not be appealing to many of the long-term members, and those recommendations should come from someone other than the minister. The minister will then be better able to help the church implement those recommendations.

There is no way to eliminate the stress a minister will feel when the church is involved in a conflict. The important thing for the minister is to keep the stress from leading to personal paralysis. Addressing the conflict as soon as possible is one way to reduce the stress because it helps prevent the conflict from growing larger and more unmanageable. Bringing others in to help resolve the conflict also will help reduce the stress. A minister should also encourage his or her prayer team to step up their prayers for their minister and the church. Although personalities are always involved in conflict, there is also a spiritual dimension to conflict in the church, and that dimension can only be addressed through spiritual weapons such as prayer.

10
Pressures of Rapid Change

A group of ministers had been studying the differences between the missional church and the maintenance churches most of them had led. One minister stated that if he ever went to another church, it would have to be a missional-minded church, but he admitted sorrowfully that he didn't know if he could lead such a church. He had been trained in seminary to be a manager, not a leader. He knew through his education and from experience how to maintain the status quo, but he wasn't sure he could adapt to the rapid changes necessary to lead a missional church. Others in the room agreed with him.

Many ministers who were seminary trained in the 1990s and earlier are frightened by the changes they see occurring in the church today. They read the articles about churches practicing new forms of ministry, and they can see the positive impact these churches make on their communities, but it all seems so foreign to them. This was not the way they were taught to practice ministry. This is also not the way many of their church members want ministry to be practiced. Even if they wanted to pursue new approaches to ministry, they doubt they could ever get church approval. Besides, they aren't even sure what types of changes their churches would need to make.

What they do know is that in just about every community new churches are forming that are quickly outgrowing the established churches. Even some of their members, usually younger families, are leaving to attend these new churches. Older members are in an uproar, especially if these younger families are their children, and want to know what the minister is going to do to get their church growing again.

I have met with more than one of these established churches that are declining while in the shadow of these fast-growing, newer congregations. Their members are usually frustrated and hurt by what is happening. They assure me they have no problems, and they are still doing the same things they have done for years. In many cases they can remember when their churches were packed out for every service. The most common reason they can think of why things aren't going well today is that "the younger people just aren't as committed as we were." They are convinced that if they could get a deeper level of commitment from the newer members and work harder, they could get people to come to their churches again. They are usually not encouraged by my comments about the changes that have taken place in society and in the church, and many of them are less than excited when I begin to ask them what changes they are willing to make to be more attractive to unchurched people.

They remind me of the members of a congregation that Ed Stetzer, the director of research for LifeWay, once met with to discuss how they could more effectively reach younger families. Stetzer asked this congregation of thirty-five attendees with an average age of sixty-eight to visit five churches that were effectively reaching younger adults. After two weeks of church visits the congregation members reported their findings. None recognized a church service that looked familiar to them. One elderly woman reported, "Preacher, the church changed, and nobody told us!"[1]

Things have changed in the church and society, and even fewer ministers have been told about the changes and how to address them. It is a frightening thing for a minister to realize that he or she is not prepared for many of these changes. After reading a book that discussed some of the changes taking place and how the church needs to respond to them, one minister angrily told me that she felt the author was saying everything she had done throughout her ministry was wrong. I responded that what she had been doing had not been wrong, but it might not be as effective as it once was.

How can churches and ministers better understand how to respond to the changing world around them? What can be done to make change less threatening and less stressful?

Reducing the Stress of Change

George Barna writes, "Science has taught us that every living entity is constantly changing. Scientists have even agreed upon a term to describe those entities that are not undergoing constant change. That term is 'dead.' Likewise, a ministry that aims for something other than change invites euthanasia."[2] Assuming that ministers and congregation members would prefer their churches not die, they have to then believe that change is not really their enemy but is the mechanism by which they continue to live. Change should be embraced as a friend by the minister and the congregation because it produces exciting new life. Viewing change as a friend should help make it less stressful.

Understanding the Nature of Change in the Twenty-first Century

Ministers are typically more comfortable with transitional change than with transformational change. Transitional change occurs when the church tinkers with programs and policies. Although it may mean some discomfort in the system, it is usually manageable. Unfortunately, such change does not address the paradigm shifts that are occurring in our society. The only change that will address these shifts is transformational change, which requires the "shattering of the foundations and the reconstitution of a new entity."[3] Brian McLaren reminds us, "If you have a new world, you need a new church. You have a new world."[4] The question is what will we do with this world? McLaren has an answer to this question as well: "The future belongs to those willing to let go, to stop trying to minimize the change we face, but rather to maximize the discontinuity."[5]

I can hear some readers asking how this is supposed to reduce the stress associated with change. Clearly, what I am writing about is change on a major level. If anything, what I'm describing will increase the pressures ministers feel when they think about leading change in their congregations.

Although stress levels may increase at first, I contend that ministers are better off knowing the extent of the changes they must make instead of tinkering with things that won't make any long-term difference. I know churches that have painted everything there is to paint, changed their constitutions, installed new windows, and dedicated everything that can be dedicated, but nothing substantial has changed.

Everything may look better, but they are not reaching people with the gospel of Jesus Christ. The churches are still stuck and slowly dying, and all their members can see it. Investing time, effort, and finances in changes that will not impact today's society is much more stressful and damaging than engaging in transformational change that may actually have a positive impact on the community.

An Example of Transformational Change

For the past couple of decades many churches have been involved in worship wars. These wars are often over the style of music that will be acceptable to the congregation. Members of the existing congregation normally prefer the traditional hymns found in their hymnals. They have been singing these songs for many years, and they continue to find them meaningful and appropriate to their worship experience. However, someone points out that the unchurched people in the community do not have the same attachment to that style of music and even find it unappealing. The proposed solution is to add a praise song or two to the worship service or to have the choir sing more contemporary music.

Much energy and effort is spent trying to tweak the worship service to make it satisfy everyone, but the opposite is often the result. Although some churches are able to develop blended services that are very well done, these services usually end up making everybody angry half of the time. Along with requiring substantial energy and effort, this transitional change creates additional stress for many people and usually makes very little difference in the church or community.

That same energy and effort would be better spent in creating a completely different worship experience that would appeal to the target audience the church believes God wants them to reach. Regardless of size, churches that are serious about reaching people with the gospel must consider offering at least two worship experiences each week. They should design one service to minister to the existing congregation and the other service to appeal to a different group of people.

Most congregations will find it hard to survive the next three decades, much less be innovative, without developing multiple tracks of worship: two or more worship services that are very different in style and designed to reach a very different group of people. Different tracks of worship are essential for two reasons: one, the bulk of the people no longer come from Europe, and they require a totally different style of worship; and two, the rapid change of our time has led to a continual change in worship style preferences every few years.[6]

Is it difficult to add a completely different worship service each week? Of course it is. It is a change that will affect the entire church system. Decisions will have to be made about when to offer church school. Will it be held between the two services, or will there be two church schools each going on during a worship service? How will two services impact parking? Will there be two different worship leaders? Will the time of the current service have to change, and how will church members respond to that? What is the church's target group? Are there people in the community that no church is effectively reaching? What will appeal to them in a worship service, and how will the church invite them to these services? Each church will probably have additional questions to answer before starting a second service.

Is it stressful to add a second service? Yes, but this is a transformational change that has the potential to impact the congregation and the community the church is trying to reach. Transitional changes that only tweak the system are also stressful for the minister and congregation and often provide little positive long-term effect on either the church or the community. If there is going to be stress either way, creating something new with the potential of having a greater result for the kingdom of God should be what most ministers prefer, and they will likely find it less stressful simply because the potential rewards are greater.

Understanding the Change Process

One reason many ministers find change so stressful is that they are uncertain how to address it. Their ministerial training did not teach them much about being change agents. They don't understand how to lead change in their congregations, and many of them have heard so many horror stories of predecessors who tried to introduce change that they are tempted to avoid it as much as possible.

Ministers often tell how resistant their churches are to change, but if the truth were known, most ministers dislike change as much as their laypeople do. Hans Finzel explains why: "Leaders often have the most to lose and the least to gain by revolutions that upset the status quo. Their very jobs can be at stake. Their power can be compromised."[7] However, if change is unavoidable and if ministers want to remain relevant to a rapidly changing world, they need to learn how to lead change in their churches in order to make the process less stressful.

John Kotter is a professor of leadership at Harvard Business School. He has identified an eight-step process to follow when trying to implement a major change in an organization.[8] Ministers could ease some of the stresses of change if they follow these steps.

The first step is to establish a sense of urgency. Few congregations will embrace change unless they believe there is a compelling reason to do so. A lack of urgency may well be the primary reason so many change efforts fail.[9]

The second step is to create a guiding coalition. This is a team of people who have sufficient respect and power in the congregation to lead the change. These will be people who are not satisfied with the status quo and who support the change being proposed. This will require that they have the opportunity to ask questions and make suggestions to improve the planned change.

Step three is to develop a vision and strategy that will drive the change effort. Too many ministers understand that a particular change may be helpful to the ministry, but they never take the time to think through a process that will help achieve it. People must be able to see a vision of what things will look like after the change is implemented, and it must be a vision they can own and support.

Step four is communicating that vision. The minister cannot over-communicate. He or she should use every means available to communicate the vision and the reasons behind the proposed change. If the minister is not getting tired of communicating the vision, he or she is probably not communicating it often enough.

The fifth step is taking action by removing obstacles that prevent achieving the desired change. The minister must encourage people to take risks and start thinking outside the box. He or she must challenge everything that would prevent the change from occurring.

Although every step is important, step six is vital. The minister must generate short-term wins to keep the congregation encouraged about the changes that are taking place. Each win must be celebrated, and the people responsible for the win publicly recognized. As we will see later, change takes time, and without short-term victories people can become discouraged and want to give up.

Step seven is to consolidate the gains to produce more change. These short-term wins provide credibility to what the minister is trying to do, and this is the time to use that credibility and excitement to make other changes needed in the system.

The final step is to anchor the new way of doing things into the culture. The connection between the change that has occurred and the new ministry successes the church is experiencing must be noted. The church culture is the last thing to change, and this will not easily occur unless people can see that the change that has already taken place has improved the culture.

Having a process such as these eight steps to follow doesn't guarantee success. What it does do is help reduce the stress of change by providing an idea of what must happen to increase the likelihood of success.

Change Takes Time

When ministers see how quickly things are changing in society, they can easily believe immediate changes must occur within their ministries. This erroneous belief is likely to lead to failure and greatly increase their stress levels. When it comes to change, ministers must take a long-term approach. Clay Smith believes that "significant changes in the life of a congregation usually take three to five years to put into place."[10] Transitional changes can occur more quickly, but substantial transformational changes in a church take much longer than most ministers would like. If they want to reduce their stress, they must see their work as a journey and look for short-term successes to help them move ahead to the larger vision they have set out to achieve.

The old adage of being unable to see the forest for the trees certainly applies here. Ministers can be so involved in leading change that they cannot see the short-term victories when they occur. This is one reason why it is important to develop the guiding coalition or team to assist in leading the change effort. Team members may see the short-term victories that ministers overlook. It can also be helpful for ministers to have coaches who can help them identify the positive things that are happening and assist them when they feel stuck and uncertain how to lead their churches to the next level of change.

It is said that the best military strategy ends when the first shot is fired. Military leaders can develop the best battlefield strategy they can, but when the action starts, the strategy often has to change. The change process is no different. The eight steps listed above provide a template for leading change, but the specifics will constantly be changing as the process adapts to the changing conditions in the church and community. Teams or coaches can help ministers identify the needed adaptations so the change process can continue.

During the transformation process there will be intense opposition from those who prefer the status quo. Sometimes even early supporters will decide the struggle isn't worth it or they will begin to see changes occur they had not planned. When these early supporters jump ship, a minister's stress level is likely to increase, and he or she may be ready to back off or even shake the dust off his or her shoes and move on to another place of service. The minister must resist that temptation. If he or she leaves or abandons the change process, he or she will frustrate those who do want to see change occur and give added strength to those who opposed it, thus making it unlikely any significant change will occur. The minister must accept that transformational change takes longer than anyone would like and commit to the long haul.

What If the Change Fails?

Despite the best planning and execution, not every change works out the way people would like. One church decided to offer a Saturday evening worship service, and it failed miserably. Congregation members planned for months before launching the service and believed they had developed a service that would appeal to their target group, but few people attended. They explored possible reasons why people did not respond and concluded that people in their traditional small community just could not connect with a worship service not held on Sunday. The church dropped the service and began to explore other options for reaching the unchurched in the community.

Another church in a larger community also started a Saturday evening worship service and also had poor results. When congregation members began to explore the reasons the service was not being attended as hoped, they discovered they simply had not put enough resources into it and could not offer a quality program that would appeal to their target audience. They dropped the service. Sometime later they again offered a Saturday evening service with sufficient resources to sustain it, and it is now a very effective part of their ministry to the community.

One of the keys to transformation is to not fear failure. Many of the things we attempt will not work out the first time we try them.

Nearly every great idea has to be fine-tuned at some point. We cannot afford to be so invested in our plans that we refuse to adjust them when necessary. While it is important to take a long-term approach to transformation, we also must be willing to admit when something is not going to work. We sometimes talk about the futility of beating the dead horse of traditionalism to make it run faster, but we can also beat a dead horse of transformation. If the change isn't going to produce the expected results, we must stop riding it and look for one that will.

Change Is Stressful

There is no question that any attempt to introduce change into a ministry creates stress for the minister. This stress can be reduced by following the strategies discussed in this chapter, but the reader must know this is a very brief look at change strategy. I would encourage every minister to read widely on transformation strategies before introducing major change into his or her ministry. Knowing what to expect and how to respond will help reduce the stresses associated with change.

Ministers should also know that there is stress associated with doing nothing. Too many ministers today are merely counting the days to retirement, and some of these individuals are much too young to even be thinking about retirement. They feel stuck in ministries that produce little or no fruit. Like hamsters running in their wheels, these ministers feel they are running in circles and accomplishing nothing. This isn't what they thought ministry would be like when they responded to God's call on their lives, but after years of going from one place of service to another they now believe that their earlier thoughts about ministry were just dreams.

Depression is not uncommon in the ministry, and some of that depression no doubt comes from the stress of feeling stuck in a life and role that seemingly has little purpose. Ministers must face the fact that nothing will change in their ministries unless they change. Gandhi once said, "We must be the change we seek."[11] Transformation will not happen unless ministers first experience it in their lives and then lead it in their ministries. The choice is theirs. They can either live with the stress associated with change that can produce good things for the kingdom of God, or they can live with the stress of feeling stuck in their ministries and their lives. I've lived with both, and from experience I can say the first option is by far the best.

11

Pressures of Meeting Expectations

What are ministers expected to do in the ministry? Sure, they know what the job description says, and they know what search committees told them churches expect from pastors. They also know the people they serve have more unspoken expectations than written ones. Plus, others have been speaking expectations into their minds for years. Let's look at some of these expectations.

- Their parents may have told them they are only as good as what they do. Many ministers spend their lifetimes trying to prove to their parents that they are worthy of their parents' love.
- Their preaching professors may have told them they must spend at least twenty hours a week preparing their sermons or they are spiritually shortchanging their congregations.
- Some church members expect them to lead the church in reaching out to unchurched people in the community, while others are convinced their role is to shepherd the existing flock.
- Some members will expect them to always be available in the church office. Many churches now provide the pastor with a cell phone to ensure that he or she is instantly accessible.
- Some members will expect them to preach powerful, exciting sermons the way their favorite preachers on television do. It never crosses the minds of these members that their ministers do not have the dozens of staff members that the TV preachers do.
- Some members will expect ministers to know when they become sick or go into the hospital. One man from our church seriously

cut his leg and spent several days in the hospital. He was home for nearly a week before anyone told me he had been hospitalized. I went to see him that very day, and he let me know how angry he was that I had not been to the hospital to see him. I asked if he had tried to contact me to let me know what was going on, and he admitted he had not. He still believed I should have somehow known he was in the hospital and gone to see him.

- Some members will expect them to be wise counselors, with insight on everything from repairing broken marriages to the best time to prune rose bushes. Such people will hold ministers responsible if they can't fix whatever is broken.

- Some members will have very definite expectations about ministers' families, their dress, their attitudes, and their involvement in church life. Many will expect ministers' families to be perfect models for all other families.

- Somewhere deep within is another voice telling ministers that they really should be spending more time in prayer.

A minister once wrote in his journal,

If I wanted to drive a manager in the business community up the wall, I'd make him responsible for the success of an organization but give him no authority. I'd provide him with unclear goals, ones the organization didn't completely agree to. I'd ask him to provide a service of an ill-defined nature, apply a body of knowledge having few absolutes and staff his organization with only volunteers who donated just a few hours a week at the most. I'd expect him to work 10 to 12 hours per day and have his work evaluated by a committee of 300 to 500 amateurs. I'd call him a minister and make him accountable to God.[1]

We've not even addressed the expectations that the minister has for his or her own ministry or the expectations that the minister's family has for that relationship. Many ministers have gone into the ministry with expectations of what ministry would be only to find those expectations quickly dashed by the many expectations of those they are called to serve. Too often the families of ministers also must live with unmet expectations until the minister is forced to choose between remaining in the ministry or leaving it to save his or her marriage and family.

The stresses related to trying to meet the myriad of expectations that exist within a congregation may be the primary cause of ministers leaving the ministry today. No one person is skilled at doing the many things people expect, and stress levels really increase when ministers try.

Reducing the Stress of Expectations

The place to start is with the minister. He or she must know his or her strengths and areas of giftedness. There are many assessment and diagnostic tools available to assist the minister in determining these areas of ministry strengths. Many of these can now be taken online at minimal cost. Some simple spiritual gift assessment tools can be self-given and evaluated. Other tools must be given by someone trained in reading them.

Ministers must also identify the things about ministry that fuel their passion. Their areas of giftedness will likely show up on the list of ministry responsibilities about which they are most passionate. My spiritual gifts are preaching, teaching, and leadership. I am most energized when I am on a church platform delivering a sermon that I believe has the potential to change lives. I enjoy leading workshops for ministers and lay leaders that will add value to their ministries. I enjoy the study and preparation that goes into developing a new sermon or presentation. Since 2000 I have found writing to be an exciting part of my ministry because I can touch people all over the world with my thoughts. For a person who spent his entire pastoral ministry serving a small bivocational church, I never could have imagined at the beginning of my pastoral work the role writing would play in my teaching ministry.

There are many aspects of ministry I do not enjoy, and my ministry effectiveness is reduced if I have to spend much time in those areas. For example, I am terrible with details. I am not a good administrator. I tend to see the larger picture of what needs to happen, but I must have others handle the details to enable our ministry to achieve that larger vision. I could not function well in a ministry that expected me to be a micromanager.

The Gallup Organization surveyed one hundred and ninety-eight thousand employees in thirty-six companies and found that only 20 percent of these employees believe their strengths are being utilized every day at work.[2] Think of the inefficiencies that exist within those companies. If these people could work more in the areas of their strengths, their companies could see productivity skyrocket. Why can't we see that the same thing is true in ministry? When ministers are continually expected to perform tasks they are not gifted to perform, their effectiveness as ministers is lessened and their frustrations with their work will continue to increase.

While this understanding is true, these tasks still need to be done, and this again highlights the value of a team ministry. The people a minister wants on his or her team will complement the minister's strengths. If his or her administrative skills are weak, he or she will want a strong administrator on the team. If a minister is a visionary who is not comfortable with details, he or she will need someone on the team who enjoys turning visions into reality. With such a team, all the needs of the ministry can be met, and the minister can focus most of his or her energy in the areas of greatest giftedness and passion.

Communicating Strengths and Weaknesses

Few people enjoy sharing their weaknesses with others. When I have done so, I have usually discovered the other people already knew my weaknesses long before I told them! In some cases they were waiting for me to discover them for myself.

Ministers must be upfront with their people about their strengths and weaknesses and the areas of ministry in which they will be more successful. In the case of a pastor, this discussion should occur before the church issues a call to an individual to become their pastor. Unfortunately, this seldom happens.

During the past eight years I have worked with dozens of search committees seeking to find the next pastor for their church. The process often looks like a mating ritual one might see on the wildlife TV series *Nature*. Both the candidate and church preen and strut for one another trying to show their best sides and conceal the weaknesses each has. Those in the church seldom have a vision of where God is leading them, so they don't really know the skills their next minister should possess to achieve that vision. The committee assures the candidate that the church is committed to growth and that the next pastor must be someone who can grow the church, especially the youth group and young families. The candidate assures the committee that he or she is just the right person for the job and backs that assurance up with a professionally designed résumé that lists all his or her major accomplishments since entering the ministry.

Only after the minister has assumed the pastorate does he or she learn the real expectations of the church, which may or may not be what the committee stated. This is also when the church discovers that this minister has some serious flaws, such as being human. He or she cannot leap higher than the tallest building and is not faster than a speeding bullet. The church didn't get Super Pastor after all. He or she turns out to be a normal human being with both strengths and weaknesses, and the church turns out to be a normal church with far more expectations for the minister than could ever be recorded in a job description. How much better would it have been if both parties had been completely straightforward with one another?

Romans 12:6 says, "In his grace, God has given us different gifts for doing certain things well" (NLT). This means that none of us can do everything. No minister is capable of meeting every expectation that might exist in a congregation. The expectations of some churches are completely outside the abilities of some ministers, and for a minister to try to meet those expectations will cause both the minister and the church to suffer.

What good does it do for a church that has just experienced a major split to call a minister who is a classic conflict avoider and a poor counselor? Why would a minister with strong gifts in evangelism want to go to a church that, despite saying it wants to grow, really wants to continue the maintenance ministry it has been practicing for the past three decades? Too often a poor match is made between a minister and a congregation because they were less than honest about the needs each has and about the abilities each has to meet those needs.

If an upfront and open conversation did not occur before the minister was called to the church, it still needs to happen. There must be a frank discussion between the minister and the lay leadership about expectations and the ability to meet those expectations. What exactly does the church need from the pastor? The leadership should be specific. Goals should be created that reflect these needs, and these need to be communicated to the congregation. If people begin voicing expectations that are outside those previously identified, the leadership should speak up on the pastor's behalf and remind these people what has been agreed to.

The expectations of the church should match the expectations of the minister. If there is a great difference between the two, it may be a sign that the minister should begin looking for another place to serve. This does not mean that there is anything wrong with either the church or the minister; it is just that they have different expectations of ministry. It is much better to identify this during a time of dialogue rather than after a major conflict has occurred due to the differing expectations.

Different expectations do not necessarily mean the minister needs to leave. He or she may be willing to set his or her expectations aside for the time being to meet the current needs of the congregation. For example, the minister may see his or her primary gifts in the area of evangelism. However, the church may have recently come out of a difficult conflict and need healing before an effective outreach program can be started. The minister may agree to delay his or her outreach plans and first concentrate his or her efforts on helping the congregation heal.

Ministerial Evaluations

About once a year I receive a call either from a pastor or a lay leader in one of my churches asking how to do an evaluation on the minister. My first response is usually to ask what is going on in the church. When a church that does not normally conduct pastoral evaluations suddenly asks how to do one, that usually means someone in the church is upset about something. An evaluation done under those circumstances is so subjective that it is of little value except to be used as a tool against the minister. My second question is, What will be the criteria for the evaluation? The caller usually admits that he or she doesn't know what criteria to use and that the church is hoping I might have some forms that other churches use.

There is nothing wrong with pastoral evaluations if they evaluate the progress of previously agreed-to goals. If the lay leadership and minister have discussed the current needs of the church and established goals in writing that address those needs, then the church can evaluate the minister by how well he or she has accomplished those goals. In addition to evaluating the minister's progress on the goals, Jill Hudson has identified twelve characteristics of an effective twenty-first-century minister that can also be part of the evaluation.[3] These examine not only ministry roles performed by the minister but also self-care issues such as taking days off and maintaining a healthy diet and weight. In the appendix of her book there are evaluation forms the minister can use for self-examination and another form a review committee can use.

If the minister is going to be evaluated on the goals agreed to by the minister and lay leadership, then the church should also be evaluated on its involvement in achieving these goals. Churches are sometimes quick to ask how they can evaluate their ministers, but I've never had a church call and ask for assistance in doing the evaluation. Ministers can provide training and encourage the congregation to be involved in different aspects of ministry, but that does not mean the congregation will respond.

One church wanted to start an outreach program that would include a number of people doing visitation one night a week. For the first few weeks a number of teams went into the neighborhood calling on people who lived in the community and those who had recently visited the church. However, after a few weeks the number of people who showed up for the visitation began to decline until only the minister and one other lay leader were still engaged in the task. Should the minister be evaluated for the effectiveness of this outreach program? Perhaps, but so should the congregation members. They were the ones who said they wanted this, and they were the ones who stopped showing up to support it.

Family Expectations

Regardless of a person's profession or calling, there will be times when his or her work will interfere with family expectations. The problem occurs when the expectations of the church consistently override the expectations of the family. When the minister is too busy doing ministry to have a day off each week, an evening a week to spend with his or her spouse, or time to attend a child's recital or sports activity, he or she is too busy.

Why is it that ministers typically work fifty-five hours per week and more taking valuable time from their families? Some ministers are workaholics who have their own inner need to work long hours, but much of it is due to the unrealistic expectations of the ministries they serve. John LaRue has found that pastors who work fifty hours a week or less are 35 percent more likely to be terminated.[4] Churches expect their ministers to be busy, and if the minister is going to fulfill even half of the congregation's expectations, he or she will be working far more than fifty hours a week.

But what does that do to the expectations of the minister's family? Do they not have a right to expect that he or she will be a loving spouse and parent? Should they not expect to receive more than the crumbs of the minister's time after he or she has spent a hard day trying to meet the expectations of everyone else? Any minister who is unsure how to answer these questions should go back and reread chapter 1. A minister should keep in mind that his or her family is a gift from God just as the church the minister serves is God's gift. The church will likely have many pastors, but the minister's mate and children will have only the minister as a spouse and parent. They deserve to have their needs met as well.

The Minister's Expectations

What about the minister's expectations and needs? The minister has a right to work in the areas of his or her gifts and passions. After all, that is why God gave him or her those gifts and passions. It is in those areas where the minister will find the most fulfillment and the greatest successes. Ministry will often be difficult and challenging, but it should not be a burden. It will be a burden if ministers are constantly forced to meet everyone else's expectations for their ministry while ignoring their own. A minister can ease the pressures of unrealistic expectations by following the recommendations in this chapter about working more in the areas of his or her giftedness and calling.

However, we would be remiss if we did not recognize that the unrealistic expectations sometimes come from the minister. There are many reasons a person goes into the ministry. The best reason is that the individual is certain that God has called him or her into ministry, but we must be honest enough to admit that many people enter ministry to satisfy their own needs.

A person may have such a poor self-image that he or she needs to be needed by other people, and ministry is a place where people want the presence of a minister during some of their most difficult times in life. Ministers that need to be needed train the people they serve to call upon them at any time. Such ministers seldom, if ever, refuse to do anything they are asked to do. The minister has imposed on himself or herself unrealistic expectations to be immediately available to anyone, and he or she trains congregation members to expect that of their minister as well.

Other ministers enter ministry because they were the heroes of the family, and they need a role that will perpetuate that. They see the ministry as a high and noble calling, and their entry into the ministry demonstrates to everyone their unique level of commitment to this calling. Such ministers can develop such a sense of having been set apart to this "higher calling" that they can almost begin to see themselves as having godlike tendencies.[5] If a minister begins to view his or her work in this manner, that minister is likely to also develop unrealistic expectations of infallibility. No one can live with the stress of having to be flawless in everything he or she does.

It was mentioned earlier that some ministers must prove their value and worth to their parents or other significant persons in their lives, and that worth is proven by what they do. Thus they must work harder than the next person and achieve more than others or their self-worth is diminished. This sets up unrealistic expectations that can demand more of ministers than they are capable of giving.

If a minister is laboring under unrealistic expectations, he or she must make sure these are not self-imposed. The minister must consider whether these expectations are really coming from other people or from an internal desire to meet some personal need? If they are coming from an inner desire, the minister would be wise to talk to a mentor, a coach, or a counselor to help identify what need he or she is trying to meet and how to address it in healthier ways. In the meantime, the minister needs to begin reflecting on who he or she is in God's eyes.

Ministers have been called to serve God not because they are such wonderful people or so they can get their personal needs met. They have been called into the ministry solely by the grace of God. Nothing they have done in their lives led God to call them into ministry. God always knew their weaknesses, faults, and imperfections. He also knew their gifts because he created those gifts.

Individuals in ministry may need to lighten up a little. They cannot do everything. Someone once said that he knew three things: There is a God. I'm not God, and neither are you. God did not create ministers to be infallible people. Everyone makes mistakes in the ministry. A person may do the best he or she can do, but there will be times when that isn't good enough, and the person must learn to accept that. I heard someone say once that she had done the best she knew to do at the time, and when she learned better she did better. That attitude recognizes that everyone is growing. The work ministers do is important. They should take their calling seriously, but some of them need to take themselves less seriously. If God had expected infallibility from his ministers, he would have never called any of them to the ministry. Deep down I think most ministers know that.

If ministers stop having unrealistic expectations for themselves, others may stop their own unrealistic expectations as well. Ministers can then begin to enjoy a less stressful and more productive ministry.

12

Pressures of Time Management

I am privileged to lead many workshops for bivocational ministers, and at every gathering these special folks identify the same problem as the biggest issue they have to overcome: the lack of time to accomplish everything they need to do. Clearly this isn't just a problem for bivocational ministers. Fully funded ministers face the same problem. At the end of the day there is still ministry left to do. There is always one more phone call to make, one more visit to pay, and sermons and lessons to improve—if only there was more time.

Too many ministers struggle with the "tyranny of the urgent." Despite a minister's best efforts to arrange his or her schedule in a way that will facilitate achieving the most important tasks, interruptions keep disrupting the plans. If the minister sits down to eat a meal with the family, the phone rings. If he or she goes into the church office to work on next Sunday's message, a church member stops by to discuss his latest medical tests. Some of these interruptions are necessary and important, but many of them are not; they are just distractions from more important duties. In his conferences Zig Ziglar likes to ask the question, "Have you ever noticed that people who have nothing to do want to do it with you?" They just show up at the minister's office, unannounced, for no specific reason, and want to hang around and talk. It's no wonder the minister's stress level rises.

Reducing the Stress of Time Management

Everyone has twenty-four hours in a day, no more and no less. A person will have no more time tomorrow than he or she has today, so procrastination does not work. Like money, time is a commodity that ministers must learn to manage wisely. Like money, time can be either invested or spent, but once it is spent, it is gone forever. No one can ever get back time that is lost. Success in ministry and in life is largely dependent on how well a person manages time. For this reason, I encourage people to take control of their lives by taking control of their time.

Taking Control of Life

Almost all people have a calendar for each day of their lives. Some may use a paper calendar, a PDA, or a smartphone, or some may keep a calendar in their heads, but most people have one. People must decide who they will let write in their calendars. Either a person takes control of his or her calendar or someone else will, and whoever controls a person's calendar controls that person's life.

In my work as an area minister our staff sets aside part of a staff meeting in November of each year to prepare a yearly calendar. On that calendar we record such things as monthly staff meetings and other activities that occur throughout the year. We record those dates in our personal calendars and know that we cannot schedule other things for those dates. I then look at the upcoming activities of the area I serve and schedule those activities onto my calendar. That will include our annual area meeting, regularly scheduled pastors' gatherings, and a few other events. These are all things I must commit to in order to do my job. The rest of the calendar is mine, and I control what goes on the other dates.

As I write this, I have several speaking engagements scheduled at different places in the country. Those dates, including travel days, are recorded in the calendar. I am currently working on a doctorate, and I have those class dates for this year written in the calendar. My wife and I have discussed some vacation plans, and those are already recorded. I serve on an advisory council for a university, and I write the meeting dates for that council on my calendar a year in advance. Now I know what individual dates I have free for the other things I need to do.

Because my wife works and her days off change, some weeks I do not write in a day off until her schedule comes out each month. I try to schedule my days off to coincide with hers so we can do things together. As soon as I know what days she'll have off, I write them in my calendar, and only a true emergency takes precedence over those days.

At this point I am free to make appointments with churches and people who need to meet with me. I can block out time for study, for exercise, and for margin. One of the mistakes people make is filling their schedules so full that they leave no time for emergencies. They need to block out free time on their schedules so that when a true emergency does happen, they have a place to shift some less urgent tasks so they can respond to the emergency.

Clearly, taking control of the calendar does enable a person to take control of his or her life. I am free to respond to the needs of people, but unless it is a true emergency, I can do so convenient to my schedule. If a person wants to know real stress and chaos, that person should live without controlling his or her schedule. As observed earlier, others will quickly fill up that schedule with their own needs and wants.

Three Questions

As a young minister John Maxwell realized that he was spending a lot of time doing things that he was not effective at doing and that did not result in much ministry success. He was frustrated and began to look for ways to improve the situation. During this time he learned the Pareto principle, which teaches that 80 percent of our success in life comes from spending our time and energy on the top 20 percent of our priorities. When he learned this, he knew he had to change the way he worked, and he began that change by asking three questions ministers need to ask themselves:

- What is required of me?
- What gives me the greatest return?
- What gives me the greatest reward?[1]

What Is Required of Me?

What is required of a minister by his or her church? We've looked earlier at the expectations congregation members have of their minister, and we see here again how important it is to identify those expectations. The judicatory expects certain things of me that if I want to keep my job, I need to fulfill. This is true of every minister.

What is required of ministers by their families? Many people seldom think of their families when they think of their calendars. Attending a child's school function is just as important as attending a church board meeting. Having a date night with a spouse is just as important to him or her as having a meeting with the nominating committee. Family activities should be on ministers' calendars the same as the meetings and other church activities they need to attend.

What do ministers require of themselves? A minister should be committed to growing as an individual and be taking specific steps to do that. He or she should also set aside time for exercise and activities away from ministry responsibilities. This past summer my wife and I spent several evenings just sitting on our deck enjoying the warm weather, talking to one another, and reading. It became one of the things we both looked forward to after our evening meal. It almost became a daily requirement for us, but it was one we both enjoyed.

What is required of ministers by God? By listing God last in these questions I am not implying that he should be the last of a minister's concerns, but it does illustrate that ministers do not always consider what God requires. Too many ministers sacrifice the need to grow deeper in a personal relationship with God to the demands of ministry. That must not happen. A minister must spend time daily with God for his or her relationship with him to grow.

What Gives Me the Greatest Return?

As a younger minister I wanted to do it all. I wanted to be everything to everyone in the church and community. No was a word I did not know. It took me several years, and a diagnosis of clinical depression, to realize that was not the way to enjoy an effective ministry. I had to slow down and concentrate on doing the things that provided the best return on the investment of my time.

In the previous chapter I mentioned that my primary spiritual gifts are preaching, teaching, and leadership. These are the areas of ministry in which I am most effective and give me the greatest rate of return. My ministry is best when I can spend 80 percent of my time in these three areas of ministry. That doesn't mean I don't need to meet other ministry responsibilities, but I can't afford to spend most of my time in those other areas or my overall ministry effectiveness will suffer. It is far better for me to delegate those responsibilities to others who are more gifted in those areas so I can concentrate on the three areas that give me a better return.

However, ministers should be aware that those other responsibilities cannot all be delegated to others. Ministers must be involved in the lives of the people they serve. If some congregation members are involved in Habitat for Humanity, it isn't a bad idea for a minister to show up at a work site once in a while even if only to help carry boards. If a church has a Saturday food pantry for the community, the minister should occasionally help out. Graduation parties and other happy occasions are opportunities for the minister to share in the exciting times of the families in the church. Ministers should be a part of the happy times as well as the sorrowful times in the lives of their church members. Being present during those times is what enables a preacher to become the pastor.

What Gives Me the Greatest Reward?

There are things about ministry that are enjoyable and energizing, but there are also things that are unenjoyable and draining. I don't enjoy maintenance activities. These are often activities that must be done to keep the ministry going, but I find such activities draining. These are great activities to delegate to others who find these tasks more enjoyable because they are gifted in these areas of administration.

Many people simply want to do the things that bring them the most satisfaction, but ministers must begin with the first two of Maxwell's questions before they consider the reward question. They may need to discipline themselves to ensure they do the things required of them and the things that bring the greatest return before they approach what gives the greatest reward. Ministers are indeed fortunate if they can concentrate most of their efforts and energy on activities found in all three questions.

Day Before Vacation Planning

Zig Ziglar encourages people to follow a "Day Before Vacation" plan.[2] Why do most people get more work done on the day before they leave for vacation than any other day? It is because they identify the most important tasks that need to be done and plan their activities to ensure they complete those tasks.

Have you noticed that a person will often have fewer interruptions on the day before vacation? That is because he or she is probably moving through the work with purpose. Too often some individuals move throughout the day as if they are looking for butterflies. When people sense such persons have nothing pressing, they are more apt to spend time with them. On the day before a vacation most people have an agenda they must complete, and as they complete one task, they immediately move on to the next one. Other people sense that. Some will avoid an individual with such an agenda simply because they are afraid he or she will ask them to handle one of the tasks!

Many people will prepare a to-do list on the day before a vacation. They know the things that need to be done, they prioritize them on their list, and they move from one item to the next. At the end of the day they usually find it was one of the most productive days they've had in a long time, possibly since their last vacation. Why don't people organize each day like that?

Some people prepare their lists the evening prior, while others wait to do theirs the first thing in the morning. Hyrum Smith is the cofounder of the company that sells the popular Franklin Day Planner. He believes that a person who spends ten to fifteen minutes each morning planning his or her day will enjoy much more success than the person who does no planning.[3] Ten to fifteen minutes a day isn't much. Surely most people can pull themselves away from a television program for that long or rise out of bed a little earlier to better organize the day.

Perhaps as important as a to-do list is a don't-do list. How many ministers think about the things they should not do anymore? In most ministries there are a number of activities that continue although no one is sure why. Sociologist Max Weber commented that the mere regularity of an activity eventually makes it something that should not be allowed to die.[4] Even though the activity no longer serves any useful purpose, people are reluctant to stop doing it. The activity will often take on a life of its own, ensuring its longevity.

Things not worth doing have babies. Do something not worth doing and soon you will need to form a committee to provide for its oversight. Eventually you will need subcommittees, officers, handbooks, and guidelines, plus annual retreats to learn how better to do things not worth doing. One day a wealthy person will die and leave money to endow a university chair to teach the thing not worth doing. The possibilities are endless and frightening.[5]

When ministers identify in their ministries something that is not worth doing but has its defenders who insist it continue, what should they do? Sometimes the only thing they can do is to allow the activity to go on but without their involvement. One minister told me an organization that meets quarterly always invites him to participate. He did once and vowed he would never waste another minute meeting with that group. Decades ago this was a vital organization that did a lot of good ministry, but it has long outgrown its usefulness. It exists only because a few people have refused to let it die. The minister's reasoning is that if the group is important to its members, they can continue to support it, but he is not willing to spend his time trying to resurrect something that died long ago.

Make Use of Downtime

People spend much time waiting or between tasks. These downtimes can be used to advantage with a little planning. I seldom go anywhere without something to read. I keep a book in my car to read if I get stuck in traffic or even if the line is long at the bank's drive-through. I never go to the doctor's office without a book to read while I'm waiting. Because I despise being late to an appointment, I'll often arrive a half hour early. I'll sit in the car for twenty minutes, read, and then go in for my appointment.

If I'm going on a long drive, I'll take something to listen to on CD during the trip, such as a book or a motivational lecture. Some of my churches are a ninety-minute drive from my office, but that drive is not wasted if I can listen to something inspiring or motivating. I seldom read fiction, but on an extended drive when my wife cannot accompany me, I will often listen to a fictional book on CD. The time passes quickly, and I can be exposed to something I normally wouldn't read.

Use a Filing System

Most ministers read a lot, but many have never developed a filing system to help them locate material they may need later for a sermon or a presentation. A minister can spend hours going through books and magazines looking for the information he or she remembers reading somewhere. This is time that can be saved through a good filing system.

The system I briefly described in chapter 5 is especially helpful for me. On my computer is a folder marked "Book Notes," and in that folder are currently 120 files with headings that run from "Adaptive Change" to "Youth." Inside each of those files are quotes that come from the books in my library that I felt I might want to use later. Each book in my library is numbered, and this number is listed after the quote followed by the page number. Anytime I am preparing a message, writing a book, or developing a new presentation, I can pull that file and immediately access information that will be helpful to the project.

A drawer in a file cabinet is filled with files in which I put magazine articles and items I find on the Internet that I believe I might use in the future. Most magazines will only have one or two articles that really need to be kept for future reference, so tearing out the article and putting it in a folder eliminates the need to keep stacks of magazines lying around my office and makes the information quickly available.

When I read a book, I highlight the information I believe I will want to file. After finishing the book I go through it looking for the highlighted material, and that is what goes into the computer files. It seldom takes more than an hour to put that information into the computer, but it saves me much time later when I need that information. Some ministers who have assistants will ask them to file that material, thus saving even more time.

Neatness Counts

A cluttered office and desk will cost a minister valuable time. I know from practical experience. My desk often resembles a landfill with stacks of papers and books everywhere. There is nothing more frustrating than trying to find a piece of information that I know is on my desk and having to sort through the different stacks until I find it. It's even worse when someone is on the telephone waiting for that piece of information. Periodically, I'll clean off the desk, throw away the junk, and file the rest, and it will stay that way for a time. Slowly, but surely, the stacks will begin to reappear.

Although this continues to be a work in progress for me, one of the things I have learned from efficiency experts is to handle a piece of paper only once. Every piece of paper should either be thrown away, answered, or filed, but a person should never handle it more than once. One consultant has pointed out that every piece of paper on a person's desk represents a decision that has not been made.[6] That might account for the stress people feel when they try to work around a cluttered desk. The clutter reminds them that they are putting off making some important decisions.

Write It Down

It is often said that a short pencil is better than a long memory. How often do people forget valuable information because they did not write it down? How many good sermon ideas do ministers lose because they failed to record them when the ideas crossed their minds?

How much time do individuals waste trying to remember some detail of an upcoming event because they didn't write the particulars down?

I am amazed at the number of people I see attend a workshop without a notebook. How much time and money could just one good idea from a workshop save? A person may or may not remember something he or she fails to write down, but if that person records it, he or she has a much better chance of having that information available when it is needed.

There are many ways to record information now besides pencil and paper. Many people take a laptop or a smartphone into a meeting to record the information they want so they can print it off later at their convenience. Small voice recorders that fit in shirt pockets can record conversations for later retrieval. Some people keep one handy so they can record their own thoughts to ensure they don't forget them later. Regardless of the means, ministers should write down or record everything they think might be important so they don't have to waste time later trying to remember what they heard.

Remember the Sabbath

We have noted that time management is really life management. An important ingredient of life management is keeping the Sabbath, and yet this is something often overlooked in today's fast-paced culture. Life is lived 24/7, and there is seldom any time to think about a Sabbath. Unfortunately, many in ministry have fallen into that same trap.

God gave us the Sabbath to do two things: to rest and to reconnect with him. We were not created to work seven days a week. Exodus 20:9-10 says, "Six days you shall labor and do all your work, but the seventh day is the Sabbath of the LORD your God. In it you shall do no work." When we fail to keep the Sabbath, we are saying that we know better than God what is best for us. Our bodies were created to need rest to remain healthy and to maintain our effectiveness.

The Sabbath is also a time to reconnect with God. It should include times of prayer, Scripture reading, and meditation. Part of the day should be set aside just to spend time listening to God.

Obviously, this isn't going to happen for most ministers on Sunday. For many of them, Sunday is the busiest day of the week, so they need to set aside another day for their Sabbath. Ideally, they should have a full day to give to a Sabbath each week, but that may not always be possible due to family responsibilities. Perhaps they can find blocks of time during the week in which they can rest and reconnect with God. However they do it, ministers should not ignore the Sabbath, especially if they are serious about taking control of their lives and their time.

Ministers need to educate their congregations about the importance of a Sabbath rest. Most job descriptions for ministers call for the minister to have one or two days off each week, and yet the expectations of many church members is that the minister will be available whenever he or she is needed. As mentioned in chapter 11, many churches today provide their ministers with cell phones, and those numbers are often listed in the church bulletin or on the church's Web site. The expectation is that the minister is always available to anyone at any time.

Ministers need to inform their congregations of their days off. When I was a pastor, I told our congregation that I would start taking Monday as my Sabbath, and most people honored that. I told them that in the case of a true emergency they should call me. However, they did not have my cell phone number, so if I was not home when they called, they would have to wait until I returned and listened to the messages on the answering machine. I could then respond as I deemed appropriate. It was a way to protect my Sabbath time and still be available for true needs that may occur.

Controlling People's Access to the Minister

A common joke among ministers is that the ministry would be a great profession if it wasn't for the people. Of course, ministry is all about people. A person who doesn't enjoy being with people should not be in pastoral ministry. I truly enjoy being with people and being involved in their life experiences. However, too many ministers are like a stray dog at a whistlers' convention. They run back and forth to everyone who calls with the slightest issue or question and then wonder why they have accomplished so little at the end of the day.

Ministers need to spend time with people to know what is happening in their lives and in the culture. A minister who tries to serve a church from the shelter of his or her office will soon be unaware of the cultural changes occurring outside that office and of the things happening in the lives of the congregation. However, a minister who spends all his or her time with people will soon be unable to effectively lead the church.

Ministers must have time to study in order to prepare quality sermons and lessons. They must have time to read magazines and books that have nothing to do with ministry and theology in order to remain informed about the surrounding culture. They must have time to sit with their feet up on the desk and dream about the future of the church. They must have time to pray and seek God's guidance about his vision for the ministry. They need time for their families and all the other things discussed in this book. Ministry involves many leadership responsibilities that require ministers to set aside time away from the people they serve. Despite the pressing needs of the people, even Jesus slipped away by himself for times of prayer and rest. Ministers must be willing to follow his example.

I am not a fan of everyone in the church having the minister's cell phone number even if the church is providing the phone. It creates an unhealthy dependency on the minister and makes it appear that he or she is at everyone's immediate beck and call. The church secretary and staff should have that number so the minister is reachable in cases of emergencies. If the church does not have a secretary or staff, then key lay leaders should have the number. Such a policy allows people access to the minister, while also controlling that access.

No one should interrupt the minister's study and prayer times. If the minister is in his or her study, the church secretary should take messages and the minister can return the calls later. If the church does not have a secretary, the minister should not feel obligated to answer the phone during such times. He or she should allow the answering machine to take the messages.

Whenever possible, people should make appointments to meet with the minister. This gives the minister a chance to prepare for such meetings and ensures no one comes to meet with the minister when he or she is not available.

Despite all the demands of twenty-first-century living, ministers can learn to manage their lives and their time. They will need to take control of their schedules and identify the most important things they need to do each day. That will include times for rest and relaxation. By better managing their time, ministers will accomplish much more and experience less stress, and those are two results worth pursuing.

13
Pressures of Staff Relationships

This chapter will look at the stresses that can exist between the pastor and staff persons in the church. We've already mentioned the value of working with teams to accomplish ministry. These teams can consist of paid and unpaid staff persons, and any time people work together, there exists the potential for conflict and other issues that can lead to stress. Too many pastors try to avoid this stress by doing everything themselves. They naively believe that doing the tasks themselves is easier and less stressful than trying to work with others. Sometimes operating this way is easier, but it also limits what can be accomplished.

The pastor who must type, print, and fold the church program each week takes time away from other ministry opportunities. The minister who develops the worship service each week without input from others runs the risk of falling into predictable ruts that may not appeal to everyone. No one person can consider every angle when developing a long-term vision for the church. The minister who believes only he or she can provide pastoral care to the congregation deprives others who are gifted in such care of ministry opportunities. Ministers are called to provide leadership to their churches, and this will happen best in an environment where ministers work with others to accomplish their churches' ministries.

Lyle Schaller explains why this is true. He writes, "In today's world people place greater demands on people-centered institutions than was true only thirty years ago. This often requires a broader range of specialized ministries in response to people's needs."[1] Penned twenty-two years ago, Schaller's observations are even truer today. People simply expect more from their organizations, and the solo pastor will never be able to meet those expectations. Trying to do so will not only increase the minister's stress but also prevent the church from growing as it should.

A friend of mine provides excellent pastoral ministry to his church. The church has grown to where he is stretched so thin that he lives in a state of constant weariness. For several years he has discussed hiring a part-time administrative assistant, but he hasn't done that yet. Some members of the congregation are concerned about his well-being and have asked me how they can help him. They claim they have suggested every recommendation I have given them, but he refuses to add any staff or do anything to ease his workload. The church is now preparing to move into a building program, and the additional work will increase his stress levels considerably.

Different Looks of the Staff

At one time the word "staff" would have conjured images of paid, seminary-trained ministers serving medium and larger churches. That staff usually consisted of the pastor, an administrative assistant, and others leading different aspects of church ministry. As the church grew, the number of staff members would increase to handle the growing needs of the church. However, today the word "staff" has taken on a different look in some churches.

While the traditional view of staff can still be found in larger churches, medium-sized churches often find they cannot afford several fully funded persons in leadership. Some of these churches are looking for bivocational ministers to lead their programs. Years ago Lyle Schaller predicted that churches averaging less than 120 at worship could be led by bivocational ministers and bivocational teams, and this is now happening.[2] Many of these individuals do not have a traditional seminary education, and a number of them were raised in the congregations they serve.

Smaller churches are often led by a bivocational pastor or a retired pastor assisted by a staff of laypeople who have the primary responsibility for different ministries of the church. These individuals do a great job serving as directors of children's, youth, and music ministries and as the heads of the church's ministry teams. Although they receive no financial compensation for their ministries, they are still ministers and need to be recognized as such.

While staff may consist of paid and/or volunteer ministers, there are some different stresses from working with each. There are also some common stresses that result from working with any staff of people. We will address these various stresses in the remainder of this chapter.

Common Stresses of Working with Staff

Whether the staff consists of paid or volunteer ministers, or a combination of both, there are some common issues that can create stress for the minister and/or the church. One of these is the mind-set some staff members have that their ministry is the most important in the church. Staff persons with this mind-set believe their ministry must have priority when it comes to purchasing equipment or supplies. There is often an unwillingness to share those supplies with other ministries in the church. I know a smaller church that had an after-school children's ministry that was at the center of many territorial battles. For example, the Sunday school director did not want the children's ministry using supplies purchased for the Sunday school. There were other complaints in the church about this ministry until the church finally decided to defund it.

This mind-set can also create a church within a church, resulting in major problems. I'm aware of one church in which problems developed between the pastor and the music minister. The pastor made the decision to replace the music minister, and for the next several weeks the choir was absent from the church. They were reportedly meeting with the music minister to hold their own services. In time, many of the choir members returned, but the whole issue created tremendous problems for the church. Anyone in ministry for a length of time will know of church splits that were caused by divisions between people on a church staff.

Free Riding

Some people enjoy being on a team, but they contribute little to the efforts of that team. They cannot be counted on to carry their share of the load. Others on the staff notice this and resent the lack of effort from their fellow staff person, especially if they must pick up part of that individual's workload. Free riders are not reluctant to ask for others to help them, but they usually claim to be too busy to assist others.

Poor Communication

Staff members must communicate with one another. Our church once called a seminary student as a part-time youth minister. One thing I stressed with him was that I needed to be kept informed of his plans. I assured him that I was not interested in running the youth program and that I would support nearly anything he wanted to do, but I did not want to be blindsided by some activity the youth ministry would be doing. I explained to him that the worst thing that could happen to me and to our relationship would be for a parent to call me asking what time a youth activity would start on Saturday night and I wouldn't know anything about it. If a team is to function at its highest level of effectiveness, everyone on the team must know what the others are doing and thinking.

Staff must communicate honestly with one another. Too often, staff persons will simply say they agree with the ideas of the senior pastor whether or not they really agree. This is not leadership and does not help the church develop the best ministries and practices. Behind closed doors staff persons must have the freedom to question and even disagree with one another. Once a decision is reached and the doors open, then staff members have a responsibility to communicate with a common voice.

Lack of Support for Decisions That Are Made

It is very damaging to a church to have staff persons belittle decisions that have been made even if they disagree with those decisions. It is not helpful for staff members to tell others, "Well, I didn't think it was a good idea, but they wouldn't listen to me." A staff person once asked someone in a church who he should call when he strongly disagreed with a decision the senior pastor made. That person suggested he call U-Haul, because the staff person had a responsibility to support the decisions made by the senior pastor and others on the staff. If he could not do that, then he may need to consider looking for another place to serve. I think that is excellent advice.

Perhaps even worse is the staff person who agrees outwardly with a decision that was made but works behind the scenes to sabotage that decision. Such a person will never achieve the deadlines given for the project and will provide minimal support and effort. Claiming to support a decision and then working to derail it is hypocrisy at its worst and has no place in a church leader. If, despite a staff person's best arguments, a decision is made to go forward with something, and that staff person cannot support that decision with his or her best efforts, then he or she probably should begin looking for a new place to serve.

Moral or Ethical Failures

Most ministers, both paid and volunteer, are moral and ethical individuals who would never do anything to damage their Christian witness. Unfortunately, there are exceptions. Some are predators who use their positions of trust to take advantage of others. Others are persons who failed to establish sufficient boundaries for their lives and in a moment of weakness found themselves in compromised situations. In either case, such circumstances create a great deal of stress for the church and other staff persons as they have to address the situation.

Stresses Associated with Volunteer Staff

The chief stress associated with working with volunteer staff is the amount of time they can give to their church responsibilities. If a volunteer is going to be given a staff position in the church, he or she needs to be free of other responsibilities. It is unfair to ask a volunteer music minister to sit on a couple of committees and teach a Sunday school class. In all likelihood someone asked such a volunteer to serve in a particular position because of that person's gifts and passion in that area. The church must allow volunteers to apply their limited time to their particular areas of ministry and let someone else handle the other responsibilities.

Even when they are free of other church responsibilities, the amount of time volunteers can devote to the church is still limited. Not only do they have other jobs but they also usually have family responsibilities. They may not be able to make every staff meeting and be available at every church function. That doesn't mean they are not dedicated to the Lord or to the church; it does mean they have a life outside the church, and the church needs to respect that life.

Volunteer staff members often lack formal seminary education. I have met several gifted individuals who felt called to specific ministries within their churches but felt they were not qualified due to a lack of training. This lack of training can be overcome either by the church providing that training or through judicatories and parachurch organizations that offer training opportunities. In our region we offer a program called the Church Leadership Institute, which offers two- and three-year tracks designed to develop our lay leaders and bivocational ministers. This program offers both Bible survey courses as well as classes in practical ministry skills. Since its inception four years ago, we have had over one hundred students enroll in this program. This year we are offering volunteer youth leaders four days of training spread out throughout the year to give them some valuable tools they can use in their ministries. Many judicatories are now offering such training opportunities as more churches are calling volunteer staff persons to serve in their various ministries.

Stresses Associated with Paid Staff

Paid staff have most of the stresses mentioned above associated with them as well, but they also bring other issues into the staff relationship. One of the most common has to do with the inequality of salary and benefits. Many large churches with paid staff have addressed this issue and resolved it to everyone's satisfaction. Other churches allow this situation to fester until it erupts into a major problem.

If the senior pastor has a salary more than 15 to 20 percent higher than the associate pastor, that associate may feel that an inequality exists. An assistant pastor is also likely to be dissatisfied if the associate pastor's salary is more than 15 to 20 percent higher than the assistant's salary.[3] If some staff persons receive benefits such as insurance and retirement, but these same benefits are denied to others on staff, there will be problems between staff persons.

Role Confusion

Another common problem among paid staff members is confusion about the responsibilities of their roles. This is especially true in a larger church with a number of paid ministers. Who leads the worship team—the minister of music or the worship leader? Who is responsible for training the greeters—the minister of education or the minister of assimilation? In a multistaff church it is easy for responsibilities to overlap, thus creating unnecessary stress in staff relationships.

It is common in many churches for administrative assistants to be assigned to several staff persons. How much time should the assistant give to each staff person? What happens if one staff person begins to demand excessive amounts of time and work from the administrative assistant, making it difficult for the assistant to complete work for other staff persons? Whose work should be a priority when each staff person believes his or her work is the most important thing the assistant should be doing?

Relationship Problems

Good chemistry is important in a staff relationship. Staff members need to get along with one another for the staff to operate at its maximum effectiveness. Sometimes some staff members find it difficult to relate well to others on staff because of personality differences, work habits, or beliefs. I was once in a staff relationship with another person with whom I frequently disagreed. Our personalities and theologies were opposite in many ways, and every meeting with this individual was a stressful time for me. We may prefer to believe Christians should not feel this way toward other Christians, but we are naive to believe that differences between people do not sometimes create stress.

There can also be relational issues between spouses and families of staff members, and these issues can be even more difficult to address. It is easy for jealousy to occur when inequalities of pay and benefits exist. Spouses may also complain if they believe their mates are working harder or more hours than others on staff. A difficult home life will eventually affect the relationship that exists between staff persons.

Controlling Leaders

Senior pastors are ultimately accountable for everything that occurs within the life of the church. As a result, some will micromanage everything that happens in the church instead of allowing staff persons the freedom to lead their programs. I've known pastors who prepare the church program each week rather than let their administrative assistants do it. I've seen senior pastors stand watching over the shoulders of their associate pastors to ensure the associates are doing things the way the senior pastors would do them. This is very frustrating to the associates and indicates a lack of trust in their abilities.

I was in the home of a minister of music one Sunday afternoon when the pastor called angrily berating him for changing the songs the pastor had requested for the worship service. The minister of music assured him that he had not changed the songs and that the list the pastor had given him was on his desk at the church. He asked the pastor to compare the songs that had been sung in the worship service to those on that list. After hanging up he told me that this had become almost a weekly occurrence and that he doubted the pastor would actually compare the list of songs to those that had been sung that day. The following day I questioned this pastor about this, and he denied the phone call until he found out I had been there when he called. This was a very capable young minister of music whose enthusiasm for the ministry was almost destroyed by an overly controlling senior pastor. It created unneeded stress for this minister of music and his wife, and especially so since he had already announced his resignation and was leaving for another church in a month.

If pastors are going to call staff ministers to serve in their churches, they must be willing to allow those ministers to do their jobs. Perhaps the staff ministers will do the jobs differently than the pastors would have done them, but surely there is more than one way to accomplish most tasks. Senior pastors must be willing to hand off responsibilities to their staff members and trust those staff members to fulfill them.

Wrong People on the Bus

Jim Collins, author of *Good to Great*, believes one of the important features of a top-performing organization is having the right people on the bus and in the right seats. In other words, it is possible to have the wrong people in leadership positions in an organization, and it is also possible to have good people doing the wrong things. This can be true of a church as well. Anyone who has been in ministry for long has known good ministers who were not a good fit for the churches they were serving. Nothing was wrong with either the minister or the church; they just were not a good match.

As mentioned earlier, sometimes the problem is that the minister is not doing ministry in the areas in which he or she is primarily gifted. He or she was called to one task when his or her gifts and passion are in a different field of ministry. Such persons are likely to be unhappy in their work and not nearly as effective as they could be. Everyone suffers as a result, and the ministry of the church is impacted as well. However, "If you have the right people on the bus, the problem of how to motivate and manage people largely goes away. The right people don't need to be tightly managed or fired up; they will be self-motivated by the inner drive to produce the best results and to be part of creating something great."[4]

Reducing the Stresses Related to Staff

The primary tool for reducing staff-related stresses is communication. Many of the issues cited in this chapter could be overcome if people would simply talk about them. Something is wrong when staff persons, volunteer or paid, cannot talk to each other about problems that affect their ability to minister. Too often, these issues are not discussed but allowed to fester and grow into much larger problems, at which time parking lot conversations begin to occur. These do nothing but bring additional people into the problem, forcing them to choose sides. At this point, the problem will likely become much worse, creating additional tensions in the church and perhaps causing divisions.

There must be a process within each church to facilitate communication. Some churches expect the senior or executive pastor to handle staff differences. In other churches such problems are brought before the lay leaders, such as deacons or elders. Many churches today have a staff relations committee that addresses such problems. Some judicatories have persons on staff to deal with staff differences as well, and they can be called in to assist. However, none of these individuals or groups can do anything if the parties affected are not willing to meet with them and discuss their concerns openly and honestly.

Regularly scheduled staff meetings are essential for good communication. There should always be an agenda for the staff meeting to keep it structured, but the agenda must be flexible enough to allow everyone to discuss not only program issues but also relationship issues. At least one or two staff meetings each year should be held away from the church to provide opportunities for staff members to enjoy some social interaction with one another. Family members can be invited to attend these as well so they can become acquainted with one another away from the formal church setting.

Some churches will have a staff retreat where the staff can meet and relax for two or three days at a resort, a camp, or some other place that is away from the church. This provides an opportunity for the staff to learn more about one another and develop deeper relationships with one another. It is amazing how people can work together in ministry and yet know very little about one another. Often, just knowing more about another person can prevent misunderstandings and promote stronger staff relationships.

I recently assisted a church seeking a new pastor. One of the questions the members of a search committee asked me was if I felt staff meetings were important. I assured them I did. They explained the reason they asked was that their former pastor would not schedule meetings with the associate pastor and administrative assistant. As a result there was little communication occurring in the church and even less planning. Each staff person worked in relative isolation hoping that his or her efforts contributed to the overall ministry of the church. The church was looking for more direction and leadership from their next pastor.

Why would a senior pastor avoid regular meetings with church staff? Perhaps the pastor feels that such meetings are a waste of time or that he or she does not know how to properly prepare an agenda for such a meeting. Some pastors have spent most of their ministries in solo pastorates and do not know how to relate to others in a staff situation. They are simply not used to having regular staff meetings. However, another likely reason is that the pastor is very insecure and is afraid to share his or her thoughts with the staff. Such a pastor is afraid of constructive criticism or that someone else might have a better plan to address a need in the church. Fearful, insecure pastors play their cards very close to their chests. Unfortunately, they do not understand that poor communication with staff members often generates increased stress for everyone involved, including the pastor.

Written Job Descriptions

A pastor once called asking if I had any resources he could use to develop job descriptions for the different positions in his church. No job descriptions existed for any position in the church, volunteer or paid. This was a church ripe for role confusion and many of the other issues noted in this chapter.

Many of the stresses related to staff can be resolved with good job descriptions that clearly describe the responsibilities and expectations of each position. It is even better, when possible, if the persons responsible for the tasks write their own job descriptions. They understand their gifts and passions better than anyone else, and they also understand what they expect to accomplish in these tasks. If they write their own job descriptions, they also cannot easily later claim they did not understand what they were supposed to do! Once they write their job descriptions, they will still need to have them approved by the senior pastor or other team leader.[5]

Training

The church seems to be the only institution in the world that still believes it can ask someone to do a job without requiring training for that job. Asking a person to accept a responsibility without providing any training does that person a great disservice. Leadership and ministry training should be ongoing in every church. This not only ensures that current workers are able to do their jobs well but also prepares future leaders and ministers for when they will be asked to serve.

This training should include both theological education and training in practical ministry skills. Church workers and leaders need to be well-grounded in doctrinal truth. Just because someone has been a Christian or a member of a church for several years does not mean he or she has a good understanding of biblical truths. They may be able to repeat certain terms, but do they know what those terms mean? Ravi Zacharias makes the following observation:

> The claims of Christ are repeatedly made in sermons, lectures, and testimonies, yet rarely do we explain what we mean when we say some of the most basic things. Many listeners have more of a perverted view of what it means to be a Christian than they do an authentic one. Stereotypical answers no longer satisfy.[6]

Pastors must ensure that their staff members, both volunteer and paid, know what they believe and why they believe it. I would also caution that a formal education is no guarantee that our leaders are well-grounded in proper theology. Several years ago the church I pastored called a seminary student to serve as a part-time youth minister. After a few months he told me he was resigning because he didn't feel he knew enough about the Bible to lead a youth group. This young man was studying to become a pastor, yet he did not feel he knew enough to lead a group of junior high-age students.

It is also important to train people in practical ministry skills. If a church asks someone to teach a Sunday school class, it should provide training in how to teach the Bible. Everyone serving in the church should receive training in good people skills. The church should require paid staff to attend a certain number of continuing education events each year. Ministry is constantly evolving, and churches must continually train their staff persons in the latest techniques so they can perform their tasks effectively. Training takes time, but it also helps alleviate a lot of stress.

Developing Boundaries

Perhaps nothing creates greater stress in the life of a church than church leaders who fail morally or ethically. The media has highlighted many of the high-profile cases over the past couple of decades, but for every situation that makes the national news, there are dozens of other failures occurring in smaller churches and towns across the country. Recall the cross-denominational study mentioned in chapter 8 in which approximately 30 percent of clergy anonymously reported they had engaged in sexual intimacy with someone in their congregation.[7] At least some of these failures could have been avoided if there had been proper boundaries in place.

We now live in a time when churches should require background checks for anyone serving in a ministry role, especially if it involves working with children. Such checks are relatively inexpensive and can be performed quickly. In addition to the background checks, churches should have in force written policies about ministry boundaries that they can clearly explain to anyone serving in a staff position. Early in my ministry I determined I would not meet with a woman unless other persons were present, and later I also decided I would not meet with a child alone. In the small church I served that could present a problem. We did not have a secretary, and our church was used very little during the week. However, if I needed to meet with a woman or a child on a weekday, I could usually find someone to work at the church during that time. If I could not, the meeting would not occur.

Great care must be taken when counseling someone of the opposite sex. When persons are hurting, they can misunderstand words, gestures, and touches. Frankly, many ministers are not trained in counseling and should not engage in it unless they've received training in the proper way to relate to a counselee. Such ministers should always refer people seeking counseling to trained Christian counselors.

The region I serve offers Clergy Misconduct Prevention training twice a year. Other judicatories offer this training as well. Such training should be required of every paid staff person and strongly encouraged for volunteer staff. I attended a session in which a pastor brought several board members with him so they would be aware of the importance of establishing boundaries to minimize risks to their church.

Praise

Praising someone for a job well done costs nothing, but it will often pay rich dividends. Everyone wants to be recognized for his or her efforts. What gets measured gets done is a principle of management, but what gets praised gets done again is also true—and it often gets done even better the second time. Such praise lifts the morale of staff members and lets them know their work is not only noticed but also appreciated.

Some churches have a dinner once a year to recognize their leaders and workers, but once a year is too long to wait to praise people for their yearlong work. A far better way to thank those who do a superior job is to recognize their efforts on a Sunday morning by highlighting their ministries during the worship service. A different ministry in the church could also be mentioned in each church newsletter with a picture of the leaders and workers of that ministry.

Almost every pastor will work with a staff, whether it is paid or volunteer, and any time a group of people comes together to accomplish some task, there is the potential for stress. All may be Christians, but they bring to the table different personalities, different gifts and passions, and different ways of doing things. Learning to respect one another, communicating well, and valuing everyone's contributions will go a long way to eliminate much of the stress in working alongside staff.

14
Pressures of Retirement

For some ministers "retirement" is a dirty word. They can't see ever leaving the ministry. It is all they have prepared for and all they have known. For other ministers, retirement can't come soon enough. They have been ready to leave the pressures and demands of ministry for years and have almost been counting down the days until they could retire. No matter which group a person is in, retirement will eventually come to everyone if he or she lives long enough, and a person would be foolish to think there are no pressures related to retirement.

Will the Minister Have Enough Money to Retire?

One of the first concerns when a minister approaches retirement age is whether he or she has enough money to retire. Many ministers serve their entire lives earning much less than others who have similar educations. As observed earlier, because ministers often live in the church parsonage, they are unable to build up any home equity. Not all denominations offer their pastors a pension program, and even in the denominations that have such programs, some of their churches are unable to pay into the pastor's account. Reports abound that social security will soon be paying out more than it receives unless there are significant tax increases, so ministers really can't count on social security. With advancing age often comes increased medical problems, and health care costs continue to skyrocket. A minister must begin thinking about the financial aspects of retirement almost as soon as he or she begins ministry.

Many ministers appear to lack knowledge about money matters. Seminaries may teach a minister about stewardship in the church, but few offer courses on personal financial management. When it comes to finances, what people don't know can hurt them and continue to hurt them as long as they live. If a minister is not knowledgeable about financial matters such as investing, savings plans, and credit, he or she would do well to take some financial management courses at a nearby community college. Not only will such courses help a minister make better financial decisions, but they will also enable him or her to provide better advice to church members when they want to talk about their own financial situations.

Along with their income from the church, bivocational ministers have income from other places of employment. Many employers today provide 401(k) and IRA retirement programs for the employee to pay into, often with pretax dollars. Some of these employers will even match the employee's contributions. Almost every financial planner recommends paying the maximum that a person can pay into these plans. One of the mistakes I made when working my other job was that I did not do that. I did not take advantage of the tax-deferred opportunity to maximize my investment in my 401(k), and I will pay a price for that when I retire. If a person has the opportunity to pay into such a retirement program, he or she should take full advantage of it. It may be a little painful at the time, but when that person is approaching retirement age, he or she will do so feeling much more confident about his or her financial situation.

In earlier chapters I wrote about the importance of a church paying the pastor a parsonage allowance that would enable him or her to purchase a home. As a pastor nears retirement age, home ownership becomes an important part of retirement planning. As observed in chapter 2, for many people, including ministers, their home is their single greatest investment. Some will sell their home and move into a smaller place or rent and use the equity they have built up over the years to fund much of their retirement. Ministers who spend their lives living in a parsonage lose the opportunity to do that, plus they have the added stress of having to find a place to live when they retire. This again underlines why I believe owning a home is a better alternative for most ministers.

There are many ways to reduce spending, increase savings, and prepare for retirement. The earlier a person starts, the more money he or she will likely have available when retirement comes, and he or she can reduce the stress that many feel when approaching retirement.

What Will the Minister Do?

A second stress of retirement for many people is finding something to do with their time. Few baby boomers seem interested in moving into a retirement community to play shuffleboard every day. Most that I talk to look forward to leaving the stress of the workplace, but they still want to be occupied doing something.

During most of my years in bivocational ministry I worked in a factory. One year our union approved a contract that provided for early retirement after working for the company thirty years. In 1996 I was able to retire from that factory job at the age of forty-seven. Even though I still pastored a church and was managing a business our family had owned for two years, I now had forty hours added to my week I did not have before. The first week I organized my closet, shined all my shoes, and lined them up neatly in a row. My grown children took one look at the closet and said, "Dad, you need a life!" I really did not know what to do with those additional forty hours a week. When I think of that, I consider how difficult it must be for someone to retire who doesn't have two other jobs to keep him or her occupied.

I believe that God has wired us to be productive as long as our health permits. An individual who worked for the same company took early retirement a few years after I did and regretted it from the first day. Whenever I would see him, he would tell me what a mistake he had made. A couple of years later, he was still miserable. I encouraged him to buy a fishing pole or find a part-time job somewhere. He did neither and died a several months later. I asked a member of his family if he had any medical issues. There were none. I believe that he was literally bored to death. The transition from work to retirement takes years to process mentally and emotionally, and this transition should begin at least five years out from the expected date of retirement.[1] Ministers should know what they will do with their time and their lives when they retire from active ministry.

Some ministers want to do supply preaching or interim ministry when they retire. As long as a person's health remains good, this can be a good way to invest some time. A minister's experience and lifelong learning can be an asset to a church. As an area minister I assist many of our churches when they are looking for supply and interim ministers, and many of our best ones are retired pastors. Serving in this role not only helps supplement a minister's retirement income but also is a way for that minister to continue the work of God's kingdom.

Everyone needs a hobby. I enjoy playing golf, reading, and riding my motorcycle. Others enjoy cooking or arts and crafts. Ministers should find something they enjoy and do it. Retirement is a time to get serious about having fun! Retirees can even travel and see the world. A couple of years ago my wife and I took a motorcycle ride to South Dakota. We were gone eight days and had a great time seeing parts of the country we had never seen before. On our trip we met some retired couples who were taking a month-long motorcycle ride all over the western United States.

Retirement is also a time for ministers to add to their legacy. It is a great time for them to invest some of their experience and learning in the lives of others. When we retire, I'm sure we'll spend much more time with our grandchildren. I hope I can pass some things I've learned about life to them so they can make good decisions later in life. I want to be a mentor to a young pastor or two to help them have a more fruitful ministry. I plan to keep writing books and speaking to help small-church leaders and others in ministry. As long as we remain mentally alert and physically healthy, we should never have any problems staying busy in retirement.

What About Health Issues?

Before my father passed away, I would sometimes complain about something hurting or about being unable to do some things I used to do. He would look at me, smile, and simply say, "It'll get worse." As we age, things don't work as well as they used to. It becomes easier to put on weight and harder to lose it. Our physical strength declines. Medical problems increase. While on vacation in Florida one year, I was playing with a couple of elderly local gentlemen. One of them told me I should not believe the rumors about retirement being the golden years. He said, "The only gold I know of is in my doctor's pockets." What can ministers do about health issues during retirement?

The first thing is to remain active. I've known people who retired and no longer did anything. Their health quickly deteriorated, and most did not live very long. Studies have found that even light exercise can keep joints limber and build muscles in elderly people. I know several retired persons who are members of a local health club in our community. While the younger persons are huffing and puffing lifting large weights, the older persons are riding stationary bicycles, walking around the track, and doing light exercises with lighter weights. They all talk about how much better they feel after a workout. A person does not have to join a health club to exercise. Walking around the community can provide health benefits. Climbing a flight of stairs instead of taking the elevator is also good exercise.

Eating properly is also important and something that some retired people neglect. It is often easier and cheaper for a person to eat at a fast-food restaurant than to fix a meal at home, but that person may not be getting the healthy food his or her body needs. An individual must also resist the urge to snack all the time while seldom eating a balanced meal. Eating the right kinds of foods can help a person avoid weight problems, as well as keep his or her body functioning as it should.

Regular checkups are essential for detecting problems at the earliest stage. Many communities have health-screening opportunities that are very inexpensive. My doctor encourages me to have my blood work done at these health screenings and to bring him the results. He gets the information he needs, and I save a lot of money by not having the tests done in the hospital lab.

Where Will the Minister Live?

Some ministers spend their entire lives living in church parsonages. When they retire, they have to find another place to live, and for some this can be a very stressful transition. Others do not find it so stressful because this gives them an opportunity to move closer to family. In our mobile society it is not uncommon for children to move some distance from their homes. Retirement can mean an opportunity to move closer to children or (even better) grandchildren.

Sometimes ministers remain in the community where they retire. Perhaps their children did not move very far away. They may own their own homes and do not want to move. Not having to move can help ease some of the stress of retirement, since ministers don't have to leave friends and neighbors, but it can also create some additional stresses that we will address in the next section.

How Will the Minister Relate to Former Church Members?

If retired ministers choose to remain in the communities of their last pastorates, they will regularly come into contact with members of the churches from which they retired. How should a minister relate to these people? What happens when the people come asking the minister to do funerals or weddings? How does the retired minister respond when they come with concerns about the church or the new pastor? Where does the minister and spouse worship? What does the minister do when he or she disagrees with things happening at the church?

When I left the church I served for twenty years, my wife and I did not move from the community, and I've had to face each of these questions. Although I entered into a new ministry, I had invested two decades of my life in that church and the people who attended there. My wife and I appreciated the opportunity to remain in the community where we were both raised, but we paid a price in the relationships we had with our former church members.

In my final sermon to the church I told the people that although I would remain in the area, I would not do weddings or funerals for persons in the church. Providing those ministries would be the next pastor's responsibility and the way he or she would effectively become their pastor. The only exception I would consider is if the pastor asked for my assistance. Since leaving that church in 2001 I have done one funeral for a member, and that occurred because the pastor had to be away and asked me to do it. There have been funerals and weddings I would like to have done, but that would have been ethically wrong. I appreciate the families not asking me to officiate at those services but instead had their new pastor do them.

Because of some issues in the church, some people chose to leave. These were people with whom I was very close. Seeing that happen was painful for me, but as the former pastor I could not interfere with what went on in the church. Our denomination asks our pastors to sign a code of ethics that includes the following: "I will, upon my resignation or retirement, sever my ministerial leadership relations with my former constituents, and will not make ministerial contacts in the field of another ministerial leader without his/her request and/or consent."[2] As much as I may have wanted to step in and address the issues dividing my previous church, I could not do so.

A minister can choose to remain in the community, but there will be a cost. If a minister chooses to maintain a distance from his or her former congregation members, especially when they go through hard times, some will misinterpret that as a lack of caring. Some will think if their former minister would get involved, their problems would go away. The former minister may think that too. I know I did, but I also knew the church members had to work through their issues themselves. If God wanted me to continue helping them through their difficulties, he would not have led me to a different ministry.

However, there are also advantages to remaining in the community and maintaining friendships that are already established. One of my final comments in my last sermon was, "I will soon walk out the front door. I can never again be your pastor, but I will always be your friend." My wife and I have been able to maintain friendships with several couples from the church. I play golf occasionally with some of them, and we occasionally go out to eat with others. It has been good not to have to abandon these relationships by moving away.

Where Will the Minister Worship?

Is it possible for a retired minister to remain in the church he or she previously served? In most cases it is probably best if the minister does not continue to worship in that church. I was once being considered for the pastorate of a church in a nearby state. I decided to drive by the church to see what the facilities looked like before my initial interview. On the side of the building was a sign indicating the parking space was reserved for Dr. _____. During my discussion with the search committee, I learned that this individual was the previous pastor who had led that church for several decades and that he would continue to be a member of that church. Since that was the only reserved space in the parking lot, I didn't have a difficult time guessing who the real pastor of that church would be regardless of whom the committee called to be the pastor. I declined the opportunity to be a candidate.

Oddly enough, my wife and I continued our membership at the church I served before accepting my current ministry. When the members learned we would continue to live in the community, they asked us to keep our membership in that church. Because my work as an area resource minister causes me to be in a different church almost every week, we agreed to remain members of the church. As I told them, we were about to become the kind of church members I had preached against for twenty years! We would probably only show up on Christmas and Easter. But I also told them that if I could not keep my nose out of issues in the church, we would immediately move our membership elsewhere.

The retired minister and spouse must not forsake regular worship. A retired minister of music once told me that he and his wife seldom attended church services. Upon retirement they had purchased a recreational vehicle and spent much of their time traveling the country, since they had little time for travel while serving the church. He felt he had spent enough time in church. There is certainly nothing wrong with travel, but a person can still find a place to worship while on the road. When we are on vacation, I enjoy picking a church in the yellow pages to attend just to experience different worship settings.

Worship isn't about how many hours in our lives we spend in church. It is about setting aside some time each week to experience God's presence and to hear the words of hope that flow from the Scriptures. Our souls need that on a regular basis, and retired ministers should know that better than anyone.

Finding a new place of worship also enables retired ministers to make new friendships, and these will become important as they grow older. A person's existing circle of friends and family will grow smaller as people begin to pass away, and he or she will need to replace old relationships with new ones. Some of those relationships will be found by selecting a new congregation in which to worship.

Retired ministers should take some time to visit different churches before settling on one. They may even discover that the one they prefer is in a different denomination. Just as young people often prefer other denominations to the one in which they grew up, ministers may find appealing the worship styles and approaches to ministry found in denominations different from their own. While a church's name is important, how it ministers to people at their particular stage of life can make a great deal of difference to them.

How Will the Minister Stay Mentally Sharp?

Most ministers spend much of their time reading and studying. There are sermons and lessons to prepare, so they spend time in commentaries to help them better understand the biblical texts. Journals and other books help ministers understand the changes taking place in society and what those changes mean to the ministry. Many ministers pursue advanced degrees that require not only great amounts of reading but also the ability to digest that reading and write reports and theses on it. All this mental exercise, as overwhelming as it may be, does help keep ministers mentally sharp.

Alzheimer's disease and dementia are concerns for anyone approaching retirement age. Although nothing can guarantee that a person can avoid either of these problems, remaining active and using the mind does seem to help. A study done by the Albert Einstein College of Medicine in New York of 469 people over the age of seventy-five found that the people who read, played board games, worked crossword puzzles, or played a musical instrument were less likely to develop dementia than those who did not do those things.[3] It would appear to be a mistake to stop reading or exercising the mind if a person wants to stay mentally sharp in his or her retirement years.

When a person retires from the ministry, he or she may want to learn about something other than ministry or religious studies. A friend of mine is thinking about pursuing another master's degree in something other than ministry just to learn something new. The pursuit of new knowledge doesn't have to lead to another degree. I know a retired minister approaching his nineties who recently took a language course. His study not only enabled him to learn a new language so he could communicate with people moving into the community but also helped him remain mentally sharp.

Another way to remain mentally sharp is to stay connected with young people. Young people in the twenty-first century stay on the cutting edge of new technology and information, and they enjoy passing on that information. Two years ago three of our grandchildren were going to spend a week with us. I knew how much they enjoyed video games, so I purchased a PlayStation 2 and a couple of games suitable for their ages. They taught me how to use the controls, and we had a great time playing the video games that week. Sometimes I'll play the games by myself just to wind down after a busy day, and I believe they help a person's alertness and eye-hand coordination.

How Will the Minister Deal with Growing Older?

Turning forty did not bother me. Turning fifty did not bother me. As I write this, I am a few months from my sixtieth birthday, and it is bothering me. I am aware that I am not handling this next birthday well, and so is my wife! I remember a comic many years ago who used to tell the story of an old man walking down the street. He saw a little boy sitting on the curb crying. He asked, "Little boy, why are you crying?" The little boy answered, "Because I can't do what the big boys do." The comic then said, "The old man cried too." I used to laugh at that joke, but now I feel like the old man!

Some people approach retirement and aging with much anxiety and resentment. Some people become increasingly bitter about the changes occurring in their lives, especially if they begin to need assistance to do things for themselves. Many formerly independent people resent having to depend on others to take them to the store or cook their meals for them. They may have no choice, but they accept the assistance with resentment and anger. Such situations can create a lot of emotional and psychological problems for the individual and for the family members providing the assistance.

How much better it will be if a person can accept the limitations that often come with aging. I can't do some of the things I could do twenty and thirty years ago. But there are things I can do today that I couldn't do then because I didn't know how. I would have never thought about writing a book back then, but writing has become something I enjoy very much. I never led workshops and seminars twenty years ago, but today I get a chance to share my experience and learning with a wide variety of people. Back then I pastored a church, worked a full-time job, went to school, and helped raise a family. There wasn't much time for travel then, but my wife and I now have the opportunity to travel more and see things we never expected we would see. I would expect that when we do retire, we will travel even more.

Retirement can be a great time of life if people avoid boredom and feeling sorry for themselves. As the apostle Paul neared the end of his life, he was able to write, "I have fought the good fight, I have finished the race, I have kept the faith" (2 Tim. 4:7). Bob Buford calls this running through the tape. In his book *Finishing Well* he interviews sixty people to discover how they approached their lives and their retirements. He writes,

> They don't intend to waste even an ounce of the precious gifts they have been given. Why should they miss out on the exhilaration of feeling the wind in their face as they sprint toward the finish line? Where's the joy in listening to the creak of the rocking chair while watching the road for the undertaker to arrive? Why turn off the ig-

nition and just rust out? Instead these dynamic personalities chose to let the odometer spin as long as the spark plugs still fire. Each of them is an inspiring example of lives that ignore the culture's expectations of retirement and just keep on being productive.[4]

Retirement is a chance for ministers to do some things they want to do, but it can also be a very productive time in their lives. They can and should continue to make a contribution to society and to the kingdom of God. To so a person must plan ahead and not wait until the day after retirement to decide what he or she will do. Each of the questions in this chapter must be answered before a person retires. When they are answered satisfactorily, a person will find the retirement years to be less stressful and more productive and enjoyable.

Notes

Introduction

1. H. B. London Jr. and Neil B. Wiseman, *Pastors at Greater Risk* (Ventura, CA: Regal, 2003), 86.

2. Ibid., 172.

3. Rebecca Barnes, "Effective Discipleship Program, Modeling by Pastor Key to Growing Members," http://www.pastors.com/RWMT/article.asp?ArtID=8991 (accessed November 17, 2007).

4. "A Profile of Protestant Pastors in Anticipation of 'Pastor Appreciation Month,'" http://www.barna.org/FlexPage.aspx?Page=BarnaUpdateNarrow&BarnaUpdateID=98 (accessed November 17, 2007).

Chapter 1

1. H. B. London Jr., "A Salute to the Pastor's Wife," http://www.parsonage.org/articles/married/A000000062.cfm (accessed November 17, 2007).

2. Lynne Hybels and Bill Hybels, *Rediscovering Church: The Story and Vision of Willow Creek Community Church* (Grand Rapids: Zondervan Publishing House, 1995), 44.

3. Jerry Brown, *Stress in the Life of the Minister*, ed. Brooks Faulkner (Nashville: Convention Press, 1981), 110.

4. Tim Stafford, "Reflections of a Preacher's Kid," *Leadership*, 1980, winter quarter, 56.

Chapter 2

1. Becky R. McMillan and Matthew J. Price, "How Much Should We Pay the Pastor? A Fresh Look at Clergy Salaries in the 21st Century," Pulpit and Pew Research on Pastoral Leadership, http://www.pulpitandpew.duke.edu/salarystudy.pdf (accessed July 18, 2006).

2. "National Compensation Survey: Occupational Wages in the United States, June 2006," http://www.bls.gov/ncs/ocs/sp/ncbl0910.pdf (accessed November 20, 2007).

3. "Student Information Project, Graduating Student Questionnaire: 2008-2009 Profile of Participants," Association of Theological Schools, http://www.ats.edu/Resources/Student/Documents/Questionnaire/GSQ/2008-2009GSQ.pdf (accessed June 5, 2010).

4. Mary L. Mild, ed., *Calling an American Baptist Minister: A Comprehensive Guide for Pastoral Search Committees with Step-by-Step Resources* (Valley Forge, PA: National Ministries, 2004), 69.

5. *Guidelines for Clergy Compensation* (Bloomington, IN: The Commission on Equitable Compensation, South Indiana Conference of the United Methodist Church, 2007), http://www.sicumc.org/PDF/Pamphlet%20for%202008.pdf (accessed November 21, 2007).

Chapter 3

1. Dennis Bickers, *Intentional Ministry in a Not-So-Mega Church: Becoming a Missional Community* (Kansas City: Beacon Hill Press of Kansas City, 2009), 23-24.

2. Paul D. Robbins, *When It's Time to Move: A Guide to Changing Churches*, The Leadership Library, vol. 4 (Carol Stream, IL: Christianity Today, 1985), 7.

3. Dennis Bickers, *The Bivocational Pastor: Two Jobs, One Ministry* (Kansas City: Beacon Hill Press of Kansas City, 2004), 22-24.

4. Dennis Bickers, *The Tentmaking Pastor: The Joy of Bivocational Ministry* (Grand Rapids: Baker Books, 2000), 70.

5. Chris Turner, "More Than 1,300 Staff Dismissed in 2005; Relationship Issues Again Take First Five Spots," *LifeWay: Biblical Solutions for Life*, October 2, 2006, http://www.lifeway.com/lwc/rd_article_content/0,2815,A%253D163808%2526X%253D1%2526M%253D200812,00.html (accessed July 13, 2010).

6. More information is available at the Ministry Development Network, http://www.midwestministry.org/denom-board.html (accessed July 6, 2010).

Chapter 4

1. Daniel Aleshire, "The Work of Theological Education and Your Work" (a paper presented at the Development and Institutional Advancement [DIAP] Workshop, September 2003), http://www.ats.edu/leadership_education/Papers2003Aleshire2.asp (accessed November 23, 2007).

2. George Barna, *The Power of Vision* (Ventura, CA: Regal Books, 1992), 28.

3. George Barna, *A Fish Out of Water* (Brentwood, TN: Integrity Publishers, 2002), 43-50.

4. John C. Maxwell, *The 17 Indisputable Laws of Teamwork* (Nashville: Thomas Nelson, 2001), 1.

5. Hans Finzel, *Empowered Leaders: The Ten Principles of Christian Leadership*, Swindoll Leadership Library, ed. Charles Swindoll (Nashville: Word Publishing, 1998), 11.

6. Timothy C. Geoffrion, *The Spirit-Led Leader: Nine Leadership Practices and Soul Principles* (Herndon, VA: The Alban Institute, 2005), 5-6.

7. Robert K. Greenleaf, *Servant Leadership: A Journey into the Nature of Legitimate Power and Greatness*, 25th anniversary ed. (Mahwah, NJ: Paulist Press, 2002), 27.

8. Ibid., 10.

9. John C. Maxwell, *The 21 Irrefutable Laws of Leadership: Follow Them and People Will Follow You* (Nashville: Thomas Nelson, 1998), 23.

Chapter 5

1. John MacArthur Jr., *Rediscovering Expository Preaching* (Dallas: Word Publishing, 1992), xiii.

2. James W. Cox, *Preaching* (New York: Harper and Row, 1985), 119.

3. Graham Johnston, *Preaching to a Postmodern World: A Guide to Reaching Twenty-First Century Listeners* (Grand Rapids: Baker Books, 2001), 161.

4. Michael J. Quicke, *360 Degree Preaching: Hearing, Speaking, and Living the Word* (Grand Rapids: Baker Academic, 2003), 117.

5. Thom S. Rainer, *Surprising Insights from the Unchurched and Proven Ways to Reach Them* (Grand Rapids: Zondervan, 2001), 219.

6. Quicke, *360 Degree Preaching*, 138.

Chapter 6

1. Maxwell, *The 21 Irrefutable Laws of Leadership*, 99.

2. Paul D. Borden, *Hit the Bullseye: How Denominations Can Aim the Congregation at the Mission Field*, The Convergence eBook Series, ed. Tom Bandy and Bill Easum (Nashville: Abingdon Press, 2003), 21.

3. Ron Blake, *The Pastor's Guide to Effective Ministry* (Kansas City: Beacon Hill Press of Kansas City, 2002), 101.

Chapter 7

1. George Barna, "Pastors Feel Confident in Ministry, But Many Struggle in Their Interaction with Others," The Barna Update, July 10, 2006, http://barna.org/Flex-Page.aspx?Page=BarnaUpdateNarrow&BarnaUpdateID=216&P (accessed December 8, 2007).

2. "Over Half of Clergy Wives Feel Overworked and Isolated," *Christian Today*, January 30, 2006, http://www.christiantoday.co.uk/article/over.half.of.clergy.wives.feel.overworked.and.isolated./5157.htm (accessed July 6, 2010).

3. David Mace and Vera Mace, *What's Happening to Clergy Marriages?* (Nashville: Abingdon Press, 1980), 43.

4. Amy Frykholm, "Addictive Behavior: Pastors and Pornography," *Christian Century Magazine*, September 4, 2007. Http://www.christiancentury.org/article.lasso?id=3629 (accessed December 8, 2007).

5. Karen A. McClintock, *Preventing Sexual Abuse in Congregations: A Resource for Leaders* (Herndon, VA: The Alban Institute, 2004), 111-12.

6. James M. Kouzes and Barry Z. Posner, *Encouraging the Heart: A Leader's Guide to Rewarding and Recognizing Others* (San Francisco: Jossey-Bass, 1999), 84.

7. Neil Cole, *Organic Church: Growing Faith Where Life Happens* (San Francisco: Jossey-Bass, 2005), xxvii.

Chapter 8

1. J. Oswald Sanders, *Spiritual Leadership* (Chicago: Moody Press, 1967), 107.

2. Archibald D. Hart, *Coping with Depression in the Ministry and Other Helping Professions* (Dallas: Word Publishing, 1984), 17.

3. Ibid., 18.

4. Ibid., 37.

5. David J. Wood, "Exit Interview: Why Pastors Leave," review of *Pastors in Transition: Why Clergy Leave Local Church Ministry*, by Dean R. Hoge and Jacqueline E. Wenger, *Christian Century Magazine*, December 13, 2005, http://www.christiancentury.org/article.lasso?id=1572 (accessed December 17, 2007).

6. Ibid.

7. McClintock, *Preventing Sexual Abuse in Congregations*, 106.

8. John Maxwell, *Partners in Prayer: How to Revolutionize Your Church with a Team Prayer Strategy* (Nashville: Thomas Nelson, 1996), 3.

9. Eugene H. Peterson, *Working the Angles: The Shape of Pastoral Integrity* (Grand Rapids: William B. Eerdmans Publishing Company, 1987), 167.

10. Ibid., 150.

Chapter 9

1. Thomas G. Bandy, *Fragile Hope: Your Church in 2020* (Nashville: Abingdon Press, 2002), 29.

2. Ibid., 126-27.

3. Jim Herrington, Mike Bonem, and James H. Furr, *Leading Congregational Change: A Practical Guide for the Transformational Journey* (San Francisco: Jossey-Bass, 2000), 7.

4. Ronald A. Heifetz, *Leadership Without Easy Answers* (Cambridge, MA: The Belknap Press of Harvard University Press, 1994), 116.

5. Ronald A. Heifetz and Marty Linsky, *Leadership on the Line: Staying Alive Through the Dangers of Leading* (Boston: Harvard Business School Press, 2002), 107-16.

6. Charles H. Cosgrove and Dennis D. Hatfield, *Church Conflict: The Hidden System Behind the Fights* (Nashville: Abingdon Press, 1994), 42.

7. Speed B. Leas, *Leadership and Conflict*, Creative Leadership Series, ed. Lyle E. Schaller (Nashville: Abingdon Press, 1982), 65.

8. John Paul Lederach, *The Journey Toward Reconciliation* (Scottdale, PA: Herald Press, 1999), 125.

9. John C. Maxwell, *Winning with People: Discover the People Principles that Work for You Every Time* (Nashville: Thomas Nelson, 2004), 144.

10. Ron Susek, *Firestorm: Preventing and Overcoming Church Conflicts* (Grand Rapids: Baker Books, 1999), 47.

11. Ibid., 168.

12. Ibid., 37-38.

13. Cosgrove and Hatfield, *Church Conflict*, 20.

Chapter 10

1. Elmer Towns, Ed Stetzer, and Warren Bird, *11 Innovations in the Local Church* (Ventura, CA: Regal Books, 2007), 13.

2. Barna, *The Power of Vision*, 98.

3. Loren B. Mead, *The Once and Future Church: Reinventing the Congregation for a New Mission Frontier* (Herndon, VA: The Alban Institute, 1991), 70.

4. Brian D. McLaren, *The Church on the Other Side* (Grand Rapids: Zondervan, 2000), 11.

5. Ibid., 20.

6. Bill Easum, *Unfreezing Moves: Following Jesus Into the Mission Field* (Nashville: Abingdon Press, 2001), 99.

7. Hans Finzel, *Change Is Like a Slinky* (Chicago: Northfield Publishing, 2004), 54.

8. John P. Kotter, *Leading Change* (Boston: Harvard Business School Press, 1996), 21.

9. Herrington, Bonem, and Furr, *Leading Congregational Change*, 35.

10. Clay Smith, *Inside the Small Church*, ed. Anthony G. Pappas (Herndon, VA: The Alban Institute, 2002), 59.

11. Greenleaf, *Servant Leadership*, 351.

Chapter 11

1. Quoted in London and Wiseman, *Pastors at Greater Risk*, 63-64.

2. Marcus Buckingham and Donald O. Clifton, *Now, Discover Your Strengths* (New York: The Free Press, 2001), 6.

3. Jill M. Hudson, *When Better Isn't Enough: Evaluation Tools for the 21st Century Church* (Herndon, VA: The Alban Institute, 2004).

4. John C. LaRue Jr., "Pastors at Work: Where the Time Goes," *LeadershipJournal. net*, January 3, 2001, http://www.christianitytoday.com/leaders/newsletter/2001/cln10103.html (accessed December 30, 2007).

5. Hart, *Coping with Depression in the Ministry*, 20.

Chapter 12

1. John C. Maxwell, *Today Matters: 12 Daily Practices to Guarantee Tomorrow's Success* (New York: Warner Faith, 2004), 71.

2. Zig Ziglar, *Better than Good: Creating a Life You Can't Wait to Live* (Nashville: Integrity, 2006), 125.

3. Hyrum W. Smith, *The 10 Natural Laws of Successful Time and Life Management: Proven Strategies for Increased Productivity and Inner Peace* (New York: Warner Books, 1994), 98.

4. B. Eugene Griessman, *Time Tactics of Very Successful People* (New York: McGraw-Hill, 1994), 87.

5. Ibid., 88.

6. Ibid., 21.

Chapter 13

1. Lyle E. Schaller, "Act Your Size!" *Church Management* (March 1988), 42.

2. Lyle E. Schaller, *Innovations in Ministry: Models for the 21st Century* (Nashville: Abingdon Press, 1994), 21.

3. Gary L. McIntosh, *Staff Your Church for Growth: Building Team Ministry in the 21st Century* (Grand Rapids: Baker Books, 2000), 161.

4. Jim Collins, *Good to Great: Why Some Companies Make the Leap and Others Don't* (New York: HarperCollins, 2001), 42.

5. McIntosh, *Staff Your Church for Growth*, 160.

6. Ravi Zacharias and Norman Geisler, eds., *Is Your Church Ready? Motivating Leaders to Live an Apologetic Life* (Grand Rapids: Zondervan, 2003), 26.

7. McClintock, *Preventing Sexual Abuse in Congregations*, 106.

Chapter 14

1. James L. Sullivan, *Stress in the Life of the Minister*, ed. Brooks Faulkner (Nashville: Convention Press, 1981), 150.

2. "The Covenant and Code of Ethics for Ministerial Leaders of American Baptist Churches," Ministers Council, http://www.ministerscouncil.com/WhoWeAre/EnglishEthics.aspx (accessed July 6, 2010).

3. "Leisure Activities and the Risk of Dementia in the Elderly," *New England Journal of Medicine* 348, no. 25 (2003): 2508-16.

4. Bob Buford, *Finishing Well* (Nashville: Integrity Publishers, 2004), 229.

Also by Dennis Bickers

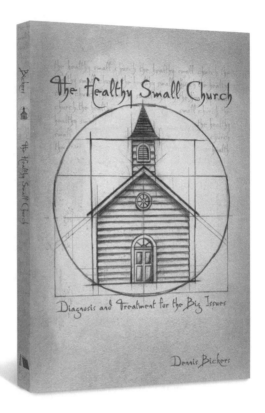

The Healthy Small Church diagnoses those things that can threaten the life of the church and prescribes practical remedies for treatment. In it, author Dennis Bickers helps your church become a healthy church that:

- Has a positive self-image
- Shares a common vision that creates purpose and unity
- Maintains community
- Practices the importance of faithful stewardship and financial support
- Encourages everyone to serve according to his or her spiritual gifts

---

The Healthy Small Church
ISBN 978-0-8341-2240-6   www.BeaconHillBooks.com

Available wherever books are sold.

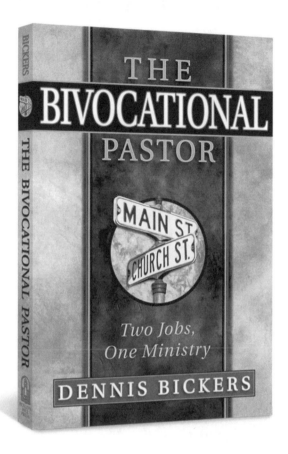

SUCCESS IN THE KINGDOM ISN'T ABOUT BEING THE BIGGEST CHURCH IN THE NEIGHBORHOOD.

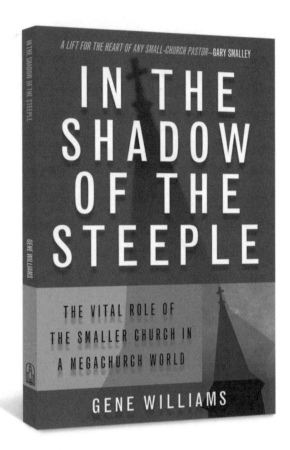

In the Shadow of the Steeple offers insight, advice, and encouragement to those of you who pastor smaller churches. Gene Williams recognizes the vital role your church serves in God's kingdom and reminds you of the unique opportunities and advantages you have to reach people who would never feel comfortable in a megachurch.

In the Shadow of the Steeple
ISBN 978-0-8341-2180-5

www.BeaconHillBooks.com
Available wherever books are sold.